The Evolution of an Empire: A Brief Historical Sketch of England

Mary Platt Parmele

PREFACE.

Will the readers of this little work please bear in mind the difficulties which must attend the painting of a very large picture, with multitudinous characters and details, upon a very small canvas! This book is mainly an attempt to trace to their sources some of the currents which enter into the life of England to-day; and to indicate the starting-points of some among the various threads—legislative, judicial, social, etc.—which are gathered into the imposing strand of English Civilization in this closing 19th Century.

The reader will please observe that there seem to have been two things most closely interwoven with the life of England. RELIGION and MONEY have been the great evolutionary factors in her development.

It has been, first, the resistance of the people to the extortions of money by the ruling class, and second, the violating of their religious instincts, which has made nearly all that is vital in English History.

The lines upon which the government has developed to its present Constitutional form are chiefly lines of resistance to oppressive enactments in these two matters. The dynastic and military history of England, although picturesque and interesting, is really only a narrative of the external causes which have impeded the Nation's growth toward its ideal of "the greatest possible good to the greatest possible number. "

M. P.

CONTENTS.

CHAPTER I.

Ancient Britain—Caesar's Invasion—Britain a Roman Province—Boadicea —Lyndin or London—Roman Legions Withdrawn—Angles and Saxons— Cerdic—Teutonic Invasion—English Kingdoms Consolidated

CHAPTER II.

Augustine—Edwin—Caedmon—Baeda—Alfred—Canute—Edward the Confessor—Harold—William the Conqueror

CHAPTER III.

"Gilds" and Boroughs—William II. —Crusades—Henry I. —Henry II. — Becket's Death—Richard I. —John—Magna Charta

CHAPTER IV.

Henry III. —Roger Bacon—First True Parliament—Edward I. —Conquest of Wales—of Scotland—Edward II. —Edward III. —Battle of Crecy—Richard II. —Wickliffe

CHAPTER V

House of Lancaster—Henry IV. —Henry V. —Agincourt—Battle of Orleans— Wars of the Roses—House of York—Edward IV. —Richard III. —Henry VII. —Printing Introduced

CHAPTER VI

Henry VIII—Wolsey—Reformation—Edward VI—Mary

CHAPTER VII

Elizabeth—East India Company Chartered—Colonization of Virginia— Flodden Field—Birth of Mary Stuart—Mary Stuart's Death—Spanish Armada—Francis Bacon

CHAPTER VIII

James I—First New England Colony—Gunpowder Plot—Translation of Bible—Charles I—Archbishop Laud—John Hampden—*Petition of Right*— Massachusetts Chartered—Earl Strafford—*Star Chamber*

CHAPTER IX

Long Parliament—Death of Strafford and Laud—Oliver Cromwell—Death of Charles I. —Long Parliament Dispersed—Charles II.

CHAPTER X

Act of Habeas Corpus—Death of Charles II. —Milton—Bunyan—James II. —William and Mary—Battle of Boyne

CHAPTER XI.

Anne—Marlborough—Battle of Blenheim—House of Hanover—George I. — George II. —Walpole—British Dominion in India—Battle of Quebec—John Wesley

CHAPTER XII.

George III. —Stamp Act—Tax on Tea—American Independence Acknowledged —Impeachment of Hastings—War of 1812—First English Railway—George IV. —William IV. —Reform Bill—Emancipation of the Slaves

CHAPTER XIII.

Victoria—Famine in Ireland—War with Russia—Sepoy Rebellion—Massacre at Cawnpore

CHAPTER XIV.

Atlantic Cable—Daguerre's Discovery—First World's Fair—Death of Albert—Suez Canal—Victoria Empress of India—Disestablishment of Irish Branch of Church of England—Present Conditions

The Evolution of an Empire

HISTORY OF ENGLAND.

CHAPTER I.

The remotest fact in the history of England is written in her rocks. Geology tells us of a time when no sea flowed between Dover and Calais, while an unbroken continent extended from the Mediterranean to the Orkneys.

Huge mounds of rough stones called Cromlechs, have yielded up still another secret. Before the coming of the Keltic-Aryans, there dwelt there two successive races, whose story is briefly told in a few human fragments found in these "Cromlechs. " These remains do not bear the royal marks of Aryan origin. The men were small in stature, with inferior skulls; and it is surmised that they belonged to the same mysterious branch of the human family as the Basques and Iberians, whose presence in Southern Europe has never been explained.

When the Aryan came and blotted out these races will perhaps always remain an unanswered question. But while Greece was clothing herself with a mantle of beauty, which the world for two thousand years has striven in vain to imitate, there was lying off the North and West coasts of the European Continent a group of mist-enshrouded islands of which she had never heard.

Obscured by fogs, and beyond the horizon of Civilization, a branch of the Aryan race known as Britons were there leading lives as primitive as the American Indians, dwelling in huts shaped like beehives, which they covered with branches and plastered with mud. While Phidias was carving immortal statues for the Parthenon, this early Britisher was decorating his abode with the heads of his enemies; and could those shapeless blocks at Stonehenge speak, they would, perhaps, tell of cruel and hideous Druidical rites witnessed on Salisbury Plain, ages ago.

[Sidenote: Caesar's Invasion, 55 B. C. Britain a Roman Province, 45 A. D. Boadicea 61 A. D.]

Rumors of the existence of this people reached the Mediterranean three or four hundred years before Christ, but not until Caesar's

The Evolution of an Empire

invasion of the Island (55 B. C.) was there any positive knowledge of them.

The actual conquest of Britain was not one of Caesar's achievements. But from the moment when his covetous eagle-eye viewed the chalk-cliffs of Dover from the coast of Northern Gaul, its fate was sealed. The Roman octopus from that moment had fastened its tentacles upon the hapless land; and in 45 A. D., under the Emperor Claudius, it became a Roman province. In vain did the Britons struggle for forty years. In vain did the heroic Boadicea (during the reign of Nero, 61 A. D.), like Hermann in Germany, and Vercingetorix in France, resist the destruction of her nation by the Romans. In vain did this woman herself lead the Britons, in a frenzy of patriotism; and when the inevitable defeat came, and London was lost, with the desperate courage of barbarian she destroyed herself rather than witness the humiliation of her race.

The stately Westminster and St. Paul's did not look down upon this heroic daughter of Britain. London at that time was a collection of miserable huts and entrenched cattle-pens, which were in Keltic speech called the "Fort-on-the-Lake"—or "Llyndin, " an uncouth name in Latin ears, which gave little promise of the future London, the Romans helping it to its final form by calling it Londinium.

But the octopus had firmly closed about its victim, whose struggles, before the year 100 A. D., had practically ceased. A civilization which made no effort to civilize was forcibly planted upon the island. Where had been the humble village, protected by a ditch and felled trees, there arose the walled city, with temples and baths and forum, and stately villas with frescoed walls and tessellated floors, and hot-air currents converting winter into summer.

So Chester, Colchester, Lincoln, York, London, and a score of other cities were set like jewels in a surface of rough clay, the Britons filling in the intervening spaces with their own rude customs, habits, and manners. Dwelling in wretched cabins thatched with straw and chinked with mud, they still stubbornly maintained their own uncouth speech and nationality, while they helplessly saw all they could earn swallowed up in taxes and tributes by their insatiate conquerors. The Keltic-Gauls might, if they would, assimilate this Roman civilization, but not so the Keltic-Britons.

The Evolution of an Empire

The two races dwelt side by side, but separate (except to some extent in the cities), or, if possible, the vanquished retreated before the vanquisher into Wales and Cornwall; and there to-day are found the only remains of the aboriginal Briton race in England.

The Roman General Agricola had built in 78 A. D. a massive wall across the North of England, extending from sea to sea, to protect the Roman territory from the Picts and Scots, those wild dwellers in the Northern Highlands. It seems to us a frail barrier to a people accustomed to leaping the rocky wall set by nature between the North and the South; and unless it were maintained by a line of legions extending its entire length, they must have laughed at such a defence; even when duplicated later, as it was, by the Emperor Hadrian, in 120 A. D.; and still twice again, first by Emperor Antoninus, and then by Severus. For the swift transportation of troops in the defensive warfare always carried on with the Picts and Scots, magnificent roads were built, which linked the Romanized cities together in a network of splendid highways.

There were more than three centuries of peace. Agriculture, commerce, and industries came into existence. "Wealth accumulated, " but the Briton "decayed" beneath the weight of a splendid system, which had not benefited, but had simply crushed out of him his original vigor. Together with Roman villas, and vice, and luxury, had also come Christianity. But the Briton, if he had learned to pray, had forgotten how to fight, —and how to govern; and now the Roman Empire was perishing. She needed all her legions to keep Alaric and his Goths out of Rome.

[Sidenote: Roman Legions Withdrawn, 410 A. D.]

In 410 A. D. the fair cities and roads were deserted. The tramp of Roman soldiers was heard no more in the land, and the enfeebled native race were left helpless and alone to fight their battles with the Picts and Scots; —that fierce Briton offshoot which had for centuries dwelt in the fastnesses of the Highlands, and which swarmed down upon them like vultures as soon as their protectors were gone.

In 446 A. D. the unhappy Britons invited their fate. Like their cousins, the Gauls, they invited the Teutons from across the sea to come to their rescue, and with result far more disastrous.

The Evolution of an Empire

When the Frank became the champion and conqueror of Gaul, he had for centuries been in conflict or in contact with Rome, and had learned much of the old Southern civilizations, and to some extent adopted their ideals. Not so the Angles and Saxons, who came pouring into Britain from Schleswig-Holstein. They were uncontaminated pagans. In scorn of Roman luxury, they set the torch to the villas, and temples and baths. They came, exterminating, not assimilating. The more complaisant Frank had taken Romanized, Latinized Gaul just as he found her, and had even speedily adopted her religion. It was for Gaul a change of rulers, but not of civilization.

But the Angles and Saxons were Teutons of a different sort. They brought across the sea in those "keels" their religion, their manners, habits, nature, and speech; and they brought them for *use* (just as the Englishman to-day carries with him a little England wherever he goes). Their religion, habits, and manners they stamped upon the helpless Britons. In spite of King Arthur, and his knights, and his sword "Excalibar, " they swiftly paganized the land which had been for three centuries Christianized; and their nature and speech were so ground into the land of their adoption that they exist to-day wherever the Anglo-Saxon abides.

From Windsor Palace to the humblest abode in England (and in America) are to be found the descendants of these dominating barbarians who flooded the British Isles in the 5th Century. What sort of a race were they? Would we understand England to-day, we must understand them. It is not sufficient to know that they were bearded and stalwart, fair and ruddy, flaxen-haired and with cold blue eyes. We should know what sort of souls looked out of those clear cold eyes. What sort of impulses and hearts dwelt within those brawny breasts.

Their hearts were barbarous, but loving and loyal, and nature had placed them in strong, vehement, ravenous bodies. They were untamed brutes, with noble instincts.

They had ideals too; and these are revealed in the rude songs and epics in which they delighted. Monstrous barbarities are committed, but always to accomplish some stern purpose of duty. They are cruel in order to be just. This sluggish, ravenous, drinking brute, with no gleam of poetry, no light-hearted rhythm in his soul, has yet chaotic glimpses of the sublime in his earnest, gloomy nature. He gives little promise of culture, but much of heroism. There is, too, a reaching after something grand and invisible, which is a deep religious instinct. All these qualities had the future English nation slumbering within them. Marriage was sacred, woman honored. All the members of a family were responsible for the acts of one member. The sense of obligation and of responsibility was strong and binding.

Is not every type of English manhood explained by such an inheritance? From the drunken brawler in his hovel to the English gentleman "taking his pleasures sadly, " all are accounted for; and Hampden, Milton, Cromwell, John Bright, and Gladstone existed potentially in those fighting, drinking savages in the 5th Century.

Their religion, after 150 years, was exchanged for Christianity. Time softened their manners and habits, and mingled new elements with their speech. But the Anglo-Saxon *nature* has defied the centuries and change. *A strong sense of justice*, and a *resolute resistance to encroachments upon personal liberty*, are the warp and woof of Anglo-Saxon character yesterday, to-day and forever. The steady insistence of these traits has been making English History for precisely 1,400 years, (from 495 to 1895,) and the history of the Anglo-Saxon race in America for 200 years as well.

Our ancestors brought with them from their native land a simple, just, Teutonic structure of society and government, the base of which was the *individual free-man*. The family was considered the social unit. Several families near together made a township, the affairs of the township being settled by the male freeholders, who met together to determine by conference what should be done.

This was the germ of the "town-meeting" and of popular government. In the "witan, " or "wise men, " who were chosen as advisers and adjusters of difficult questions, exist the future legislature and judiciary, while in the king, or "alder-mann" ("Ealdorman") we see not an oppressor, but one who by superior age and experience is fitted to lead. Cerdic, first Saxon king, was simply Cerdic the "Ealdorman" or "Alder-mann. "

They were a free people from the beginning. They had never bowed the neck to yoke, their heads had never bent to tyranny. Better far was it that Roman civilization, built upon Keltic-Briton foundation, should have been effaced utterly, and that this strong untamed humanity, even cruel and terrible as it was, should replace it. Roman laws, language, literature, faith, manners, were all swept away. A few mosaics, coins, and ruined fragments of walls and roads are all the record that remains of 300 years of occupation.

And the Briton himself—what became of him? In Ireland and Scotland he lingers still; but, except in Wales and Cornwall, England knows him no more. Like the American Indian, he was swept into the remote, inaccessible corners of his own land. It seemed cruel, but it had to be. Would we build strong and high, it must not be upon *sand*. We distrust the Kelt as a foundation for nations as we do sand for our temples. France was never cohesive until a mixture of Teuton had toughened it. Genius makes a splendid spire, but a poor cornerstone. It would seem that the Keltic race, brilliant and richly endowed, was still unsuited to the world in its higher stages of development. In Britain, Gaul, and Spain they were displaced and absorbed by the Germanic races. And now for long centuries no Keltic people of importance has maintained its independence; the Gaelic of the Scotch Highlands and of Ireland, the native dialect of the Welsh and of Brittany, being the scanty remains of that great family of related tongues which once occupied more territory than German, Latin, and Greek combined. The solution of the Irish question may lie in the fact that the Irish are fighting against the inevitable; that they belong to a race which is on its way to extinction, and which is intended to survive only as a brilliant thread, wrought into the texture of more commonplace but more enduring peoples.

It was written in the book of fate that a great nation should arise upon that green island by the North Sea. A foundation of Roman cement, made by a mingling of Keltic-Briton, and a corrupt, decayed civilization, would have altered not alone the fate of a nation, but the History of the World. Our barbarian ancestors brought from Schleswig-Holstein a rough, clean, strong foundation for what was to become a new type of humanity on the face of the earth. A Humanity which was not to be Persian nor Greek, nor yet Roman, but to be nourished on the best results of all, and to become the standard-bearer for the Civilization of the future.

[Sidenote: Teutonic Invasion, 449 A. D.]

The Jutes came first as an advance-guard of the great Teuton invasion. It was but the prologue to the play when Hengist and Horsa, in 449 A. D., occupied what is now Kent, in the Southeast extremity of England. It was only when Cerdic and his Saxons

The Evolution of an Empire

placed foot on British soil(495 A. D.) that the real drama began. And when the Angles shortly afterward followed and occupied all that the Saxons had not appropriated (the north and east coast), the actors were all present and the play began. The Angles were destined to bestow their name upon the land (Angle- land), and the Saxons a line of kings extending from Cerdic to Victoria.

[Sidenote: English Kingdoms Consolidated.]

Covetous of each other's possessions, these Teutons fought as brothers will. Exterminating the Britons was diversified with efforts to exterminate one another. Seven kingdoms, four Anglian and three Saxon, for 300 years tried to annihilate each other; then, finally submitting to the strongest, united completely, —as only children of one household of nations can do. The Saxons had been for two centuries dominating more and more until the long struggle ended— behold, Anglo-Saxon England consolidated English under one Saxon king! The other kingdoms— Northumbria, Mercia, East Anglia, Kent, Sussex, and Essex—surviving as shires and counties.

In 802 A. D., while Charlemagne was welding together his vast and composite empire, the Saxon Egbert (Ecgberht), descendant of Cerdic (the "Alder-mann"), was consolidating a less imposing, but, as it has proved, more permanent kingdom; and the History of a United England had begun.

While Christianity had been effaced by the Teuton invasion in England, it had survived among the Irish-Britons. Ireland was never paganized. With fiery zeal, her people not alone maintained the religion of the Cross at home, but even drove back the heathen flood by sending missionaries among the Picts in the Highlands, and into other outlying territory about the North Sea.

Pope Gregory the Great saw this Keltic branch of Christendom, actually outrunning Latin Christianity in activity, and he was spurred to an act which was to be fraught with tremendous consequences.

The Evolution of an Empire

CHAPTER II.

[Sidenote: Augustine Came, 597.]

The same spot in Kent (the isle of Thanet), which had witnessed the landing of Hengist and Horsa in 449, saw in 597 a band of men, calling themselves "Strangers from Rome, " arriving under the leadership of Augustine.

They moved in solemn procession toward Canterbury, bearing before them a silver cross, with a picture of Christ, chanting in concert, as they went, the litany of their Church. Christianity had entered by the same, door through which paganism had come 150 years before.

The religion of Wodin and Thor had ceased to satisfy the expanding soul of the Anglo-Saxon; and the new faith rapidly spread; its charm consisting in the light it seemed to throw upon the darkness encompassing man's past and future.

An aged chief said to Edwin, king of Northumbria, (after whom "Edwins- borough" was named,) "Oh, King, as a bird flies through this hall on a winter night, coming out of the darkness, and vanishing into the darkness again, even so is our life! If these strangers can tell us aught of what is beyond, let us hear them. "

King Edwin was among the first to espouse the new religion, and in less than one hundred years the entire land was Christianized.

With the adoption of Christianity a new life began to course in the veins of the people.

[Sidenote: Caedmon Father of English Poetry.]

Caedmon, an unlettered Northumbrian peasant, was inspired by an Angel who came to him in his sleep and told him to "Sing. " "He was not disobedient unto the heavenly vision. " He wrote epics upon all the sacred themes, from the creation of the World to the Ascension of Christ and the final judgment of man, and English literature was born.

The Evolution of an Empire

"Paradise Lost, " one thousand years later, was but the echo of this poet-peasant, who was the Milton of the 7th Century.

In the 8th Century, Baeda (the venerable Beda), another Northumbrian, who was monk, scholar, and writer, wrote the first History of his people and his country, and discoursed upon astronomy, physics, meteorology, medicine, and philosophy. These were but the early lispings of Science; but they held the germs of the "British Association" and of the "Royal Society; " for as English poetry has its roots in Caedmon, so is English intellectual life rooted in Baeda.

The culmination of this new era was in Alfred, who came to the throne of his grandfather, Egbert, in 871.

He brought the highest ideals of the duties of a King, a broad, statesmanlike grasp of conditions, an unsullied heart, and a clear, strong intelligence, with unusual inclination toward an intellectual life.

Few Kings have better deserved the title of "great. " With him began the first conception of National law. He prepared a code for the administration of justice in his Kingdom, which was prefaced by the Ten Commandments, and ended with the Golden Rule; while in his leisure hours he gave coherence and form to the literature of the time. Taking the writings of Caedmon, Baeda, Pope Gregory, and Boethius; translating, editing, commentating, and adding his own to the views of others upon a wide range of subjects.

He was indeed the father not alone of a legal system in England, but of her culture and literature besides. The people of Wantage, his native town, did well, in 1849, to celebrate the one-thousandth anniversary of the birth of the great King Alfred.

But a condition of decadence was in progress in England, which Alfred's wise reign was powerless to arrest, and which his greatness may even have tended to hasten. The distance between the king and the people had widened from a mere step to a gulf. When the Saxon kings began to be clothed with a mysterious dignity as "the Lord's anointed, " the people were correspondingly degraded; and the degradation of this class, in which the true strength of England consisted, bore unhappy but natural fruits.

The Evolution of an Empire

A slave or "unfree" class had come with the Teutons from their native land. This small element had for centuries now been swelled by captives taken in war, and by accessions through misery, poverty, and debt, which drove men to sell themselves and families and wear the collar of servitude. The slave was not under the lash; but he was a mere chattel, having no more part than cattle (from whom this title is derived) in the real life of the state.

In addition to this, political and social changes had been long modifying the structure of society in a way tending to degrade the general condition. As the lesser Kingdoms were merged into one large one, the wider dominion of the king removed him further from the people; every succeeding reign raising him higher, depressing them lower, until the old English freedom was lost.

The "folk-moot" and "Witenagemot" [Footnote: Witenagemot—a Council composed of "Witan" or "Wise Men. "] were heard of no more. The life of the early English State had been in its "folk-moot, " and hence rested upon the individual English freeman, who knew no superior but God, and the law. Now, he had sunk into the mere "villein, " bound to follow his lord to the field, to give him his personal service, and to look to him alone for justice. With the decline of the freeman (or of popular government) came Anglo-Saxon degeneracy, which made him an easy prey to the Danes.

The Northmen were a perpetual menace and scourge to England and Scotland. There never could be any feeling of permanent security while that hostile flood was always ready to press in through an unguarded spot on the coast. The sea wolves and robbers from Norway came devouring, pillaging, and ravaging, and then away again to their own homes or lairs. Their boast was that they "scorned to earn by sweat what they might win by blood. " But the Northmen from Denmark were of a different sort. They were looking for permanent conquest, and had dreams of Empire, and, in fact, had had more or less of a grasp upon English soil for centuries before Alfred; and one of his greatest achievements was driving these hated invaders out of England. In 1013, under the leadership or Sweyn, they once more poured in upon the land, and after a brief but fierce struggle a degenerate England was gathered into the iron hand of the Dane.

[Sidenote: Danish Kings, 1013 to 1042]

The Evolution of an Empire

Canute, the son of Sweyn, continued the successes of his father, conquering in Scotland Duncan (of Shakespeare's "Macbeth"), and proceeded to realize his dream of a great Scandinavian empire, which should include Denmark, Sweden, Norway, and England. He was one of those monumental men who mark the periods in the pages of History, and yet child enough to command the tides to cease, and when disobeyed, was so humiliated he never again placed a crown upon his head, acknowledging the presence of a King greater than himself.

Conqueror though he was, the Dane was not exactly a foreigner in England. The languages of the two nations were almost the same, and a race affinity took away much of the bitterness of the subjugation, while Canute ruled more as a wise native King than as a Conqueror.

But the span of life, even of a founder of Empire, is short. Canute's sons were degenerate, cruel, and in forty years after the Conquest had so exasperated the Anglo-Saxons that enough of the primitive spirit returned, to throw off the foreign yoke, and the old Saxon line was restored in Edward, known as "the Confessor."

[Sidenote: Edward the Confessor, 1042 to 1066]

Edward had qualities more fitted to adorn the cloister than the throne. He was more of a Saint than King, and was glad to leave the affairs of his realm in the hands of Earl Godwin. This man was the first great English statesman who had been neither Priest nor King. Astute, powerful, dexterous, he was virtual ruler of the Kingdom until King Edward's death in 1066, when, in the absence of an heir, Godwin's son Harold was called to the empty throne.

Foreign royal alliances have caused no end of trouble in the life of Kingdoms. A marriage between a Saxon King and a Norman Princess, in about the year 1000 A. D., has made a vast deal of history. This Princess of Normandy, was the grandmother of the man, who was to be known as "William the Conqueror." In the absence of a direct heir to the English throne, made vacant by Edward's death, this descent gave a shadowy claim to the ambitious Duke across the Channel, which he was not slow to use for his own purposes.

He asserted that Edward had promised that he should succeed him, and that Harold, the son of Godwin, had assured him of his assistance in securing his rights upon the death of Edward the Confessor. A tremendous indignation stirred his righteous soul when he heard of the crowning of Harold; not so much at the loss of the throne, as at the treachery of his friend.

[Sidenote: Norman Conquest, 1066. Death of King Harold.]

In the face of tremendous opposition and difficulties, he got together his reluctant Barons and a motley host, actually cutting down the trees with which to create a fleet, and then, depending upon pillage for subsistence, rushed to face victory or ruin.

The Battle of Senlac (or Hastings) has been best told by a woman's hand in the famous Bayeux Tapestry. An arrow pierced the unhappy Harold in the eye, entering the brain, and the head which had worn the crown of England ten short months lay in the dust, William, with wrath unappeased, refusing him burial.

[Sidenote: William I., King of England, 1066]

William, Duke of Normandy, was King of England. Not alone that. He claimed that he had been rightful King ever since the death of his cousin Edward the Confessor; and that those who had supported Harold were traitors, and their lands confiscated to the crown. As nearly all had been loyal to Harold, the result was that most of the wealth of the Nation was emptied into William's lap, not by right of conquest, but by English law.

Feudalism had been gradually stifling old English freedom, and the King saw himself confronted with a feudal baronage, nobles claiming hereditary, military, and judicial power independent of the King, such as degraded the Monarchy and riveted down the people in France for centuries. With the genius of the born ruler and conqueror, William discerned the danger, and its remedy. Availing himself of the early legal constitution of England, he placed justice in the old local courts of the "hundred" and "shire, " to which every freeman had access, and these courts he placed under the jurisdiction of the *King* alone. In Germany and France the vassal owned supreme fealty to his *lord*, against all foes, even the King himself. In England, the tenant from this time swore direct fealty to none save his King.

The Evolution of an Empire

With the unbounded wealth at his disposal, William granted enormous estates to his followers upon condition of military service at his call. In other words, he seized the entire landed property of the State, and then used it to buy the allegiance of the people. By this means the whole Nation was at his command as an army subject to his will; and there was at the same time a breaking up of old feudal tyrannies by a redistribution of the soil under a new form of land tenure.

The City of London was rewarded for instant submission by a Charter, signed, —not by his name—but his mark, for the Conqueror of England (from whom Victoria is twenty-fifth remove in descent), could not write his name.

He built the Tower of London, to hold the City in restraint. Fortress, palace, prison, it stands to-day the grim progenitor of the Castles and Strongholds which soon frowned from every height in England.

He took the outlawed despised Jew under his protection. Not as a philanthropist, but seeing in him a being who was always accumulating wealth, which could in any emergency be wrung from him by torture, if milder measures failed. Their hoarded treasure flowed into the land. They built the first stone houses, and domestic architecture was created. Jewish gold built Castles and Cathedrals, and awoke the slumbering sense of beauty. Through their connection with the Jews in Spain and the East, knowledge of the physical sciences also streamed into the land, and an intellectual life was revived, which bore fruit a century and a half later in Roger Bacon.

[Sidenote: "Domesday Book. " Meeting at Salisbury Plain. 1036]

All these things were not done in a day. It was twenty years after the Conquest that William ordered a survey and valuation of all the land, which was recorded in what was known as "Domesday Book, " that he might know the precise financial resources of his kingdom, and what was due him on the confiscated estates. Then he summoned all the nobles and large landholders to meet him at Salisbury Plain, and those shapeless blocks at "Stonehenge" witnessed a strange scene when 60,000 men there took solemn oath to support William as King *even against their own lords*. With this splendid consummation his work was practically finished. He had, with supreme dexterity and wisdom, blended two Civilizations, had at the right moment curbed the destructive element in feudalism, and had secured to the Englishman free access to the surface for all time. Thus the old English freedom was in fact restored by the Norman Conquest, by *direct* act of the Conqueror.

William typified in his person a transitional time, the old Norse world, mingling strangely in him with the new. He was the last outcome of his race. Norse daring and cruelty were side by side with gentleness and aspiration. No human pity tempered his vengeance. When hides were hung on the City Walls at Alencon, in insult to his mother (the daughter of a tanner), he tore out the eyes, cut off the hands and feet of the prisoners, and threw them over the walls. When he did this, and when he refused Harold's body a grave, it was the spirit of the sea- wolves within him. But it was the man of the coming Civilization, who could not endure death by process of law in his Kingdom, and who delighted to discourse with the gentle and pious Anselm, upon the mysteries of life and death.

The *indirect* benefits of the Conquest, came in enriching streams from the older civilizations. As Rome had been heir to the accumulations of experience in the ancient Nations, so England, through France became the heir to Latin institutions, and was joined to the great continuous stream of the World's highest development. Fresh intellectual stimulus renovated the Church. Roman law was planted upon the simple Teuton system of rights. Every department in State and in Society shared the advance, while language became refined, flexible, and enriched.

This engrafting with the results of antiquity, was an enormous saving of time, in the development of a nation; but it did not change the essential character of the Anglo-Saxon, nor of his speech. The ravenous Teuton could devour and assimilate all these new elements and be himself—be Saxon still. The language of Bunyan and of the Bible, is Saxon; and it is the language of the Englishman to-day in childhood and in extremity. A man who is thoroughly in earnest— who is drowning— speaks Saxon. Character, as much as speech, remains unaltered. There is no trace of the Norman in the House of Commons, nor in the meetings at Exeter Hall, nor in the home, nor life of the people anywhere.

The qualities which have made England great were brought across the North Sea in those "keels" in the 5th Century. The Anglo-Saxon put on the new civilization and institutions brought him by the Conquest, as he would an embroidered garment; but the man within the garment, though modified by civilization, has never essentially changed.

CHAPTER III.

It is not in the exploits of its Kings but in the aspirations and struggles of its people, that the true history of a nation is to be sought. During the rule and misrule of the two sons, and grandson, of the Conqueror, England was steadily growing toward its ultimate form.

As Society outgrew the simple ties of blood which bound it together in old Saxon England, the people had sought a larger protection in combinations among fellow freemen, based upon identity of occupation.

[Sidenote: The "Gilds."]

The "Frith-Gilds, " or peace Clubs, came into existence in Europe during the 9th and 10th Centuries. They were harshly repressed in Germany and Gaul, but found kindly welcome from Alfred in England. In their mutual responsibility, in their motto, "if any misdo, let all bear it, " Alfred saw simply an enlarged conception of the *"family, "* which was the basis of the Saxon social structure; and the adoption of this idea of a larger unity, in *combination*, was one of the first phases of an expanding national life. So, after the conquest, while ambitious kings were absorbing French and Irish territory or fighting with recalcitrant barons, the *merchant, craft,* and *church* "*gilds*" were creating a great popular force, which was to accomplish more enduring conquests.

It was in the "boroughs" and in these "gilds" that the true life of the nation consisted. It was the shopkeepers and artisans which brought the right of free speech, and free meeting, and of equal justice across the ages of tyranny. One freedom after another was being won, and the battle with oppression was being fought, not by Knights and Barons, but by the sturdy burghers and craftsmen. Silently as the coral insect, the Anglo-Saxon was building an indestructible foundation for English liberties.

[Sidenote: William II., 1017-1100. The Crusades Commenced, 1095. Henry I., 1100-1135]

The Conqueror had bequeathed England to his second son, William Rufus, and Normandy to his eldest son, Robert. In 1095 (eight years

The Evolution of an Empire

after his death) commenced those extraordinary wars carried on by the chivalry of Europe against the Saracens in the East. Robert, in order to raise money to join the first crusade, mortgaged Normandy to his brother, and an absorption of Western France had begun, which, by means of conquest by arms and the more peaceful conquest by marriage, would in fifty years extend English dominion from the Scottish border to the Pyrenees.

William's son Henry (I.), who succeeded his older brother, William Rufus, inherited enough of his father's administrative genius to complete the details of government which he had outlined. He organized the beginning of a judicial system, creating out of his secretaries and Royal Ministers a Supreme Court, whose head bore the title of Chancellor. He created also another tribunal, which represented the body of royal vassals who had all hitherto been summoned together three times a year. This "King's Court, " as it was called, considered everything relating to the revenues of the state. Its meetings were about a table with a top like a chessboard, which led to calling the members who sat, "Barons of the Exchequer. " He also wisely created a class of lesser nobles, upon whom the old barons looked down with scorn, but who served as a counterbalancing force against the arrogance of an old nobility, and bridged the distance between them and the people.

So, while the thirty-five years of Henry's reign advanced and developed the purposes of his father, his marriage with a Saxon Princess did much to efface the memory of foreign conquest, in restoring the old Saxon blood to the royal line. But the young Prince who embodied this hope, went down with 140 young nobles in the "White Ship, " while returning from Normandy. It is said that his father never smiled again, and upon his death, his nephew Stephen was king during twenty unfruitful years.

But the succession returned through Matilda, daughter of Henry I and the Saxon princess. She married Geoffrey, Count of Anjou. This Geoffrey, called "the handsome, " always wore in his helmet a sprig of the broom-plant of Anjou (*Planta genista*), hence their son, Henry II. of England, was known as Henry *Plante-à-genêt*.

[Sidenote: Henry II., 1154-1189. House of Plantagenet, 1154-1399. Thomas à Becket's Death 1170.]

The Evolution of an Empire

This first Plantagenet was a strong, coarse-fibred man; a practical reformer, without sentiment, but really having good government profoundly at heart.

He took the reins into his great, rough hands with a determination first of all to curb the growing power of the clergy, by bringing it under the jurisdiction of the civil courts. To this end he created his friend and chancellor, Thomas à Becket, a primate of the Church to aid the accomplishment of his purpose. But from the moment Becket became Archbishop of Canterbury, he was transformed into the defender of the organization he was intended to subdue. Henry was furious when he found himself resisted and confronted by the very man he had created as an instrument of his will. These were years of conflict. At last, in a moment of exasperation, the king exclaimed, "Is there none brave enough to rid me of this low-born priest! " This was construed into a command. Four knights sped swiftly to Canterbury Cathedral, and murdered the Archbishop at the altar. Henry was stricken with remorse, and caused himself to be beaten with rods like the vilest criminal, kneeling upon the spot stained with the blood of his friend. It was a brutal murder, which caused a thrill of horror throughout Christendom. Becket was canonized; miracles were performed at his tomb, and for hundreds of years a stream of bruised humanity flowed into Canterbury, seeking surcease of sorrow, and cure for sickness and disease, by contact with the bones of the murdered saint.

But Henry had accomplished his end. The clergy was under the jurisdiction of the King's Court during his reign. He also continued the judicial reorganization commenced by Henry I. He divided the kingdom into judicial districts. This completely effaced the legal jurisdiction of the nobles. The Circuits thus defined correspond roughly with those existing to-day; and from the Court of Appeals, which was also his creation, came into existence tribunal after tribunal in the future, including the "Star Chamber" and "Privy Council. "

But of all the blows aimed at the barons none told more effectually than the restoration of a national militia, which freed the crown from dependence upon feudal retainers for military service.

In a fierce quarrel between two Irish chieftains, Henry was called upon to interfere; and when the quarrel was adjusted, Ireland found herself annexed to the English crown, and ruled by a viceroy

The Evolution of an Empire

appointed by the king. The drama of the Saxons defending the Britons from the Picts and Scots, was repeated.

This first Plantagenet, with fiery face, bull-neck, bowed legs, keen, rough, obstinate, passionate, left England greater and freer, and yet with more of a personal despotism than he had found her. The trouble with such triumphs is that they presuppose the wisdom and goodness of succeeding tyrants.

Henry's heart broke when he learned that his favorite son, John, was conspiring against him. He turned his face to the wall and died (1189), the practical hard-headed old king leaving his throne to a romantic dreamer, who could not even speak the language of his country.

Richard (Coeur de Lion) was a hero of romance, but not of history. The practical concerns of his kingdom had no charm for him. His eye was fixed upon Jerusalem, not England, and he spent almost the entire ten years of his reign in the Holy Land.

The Crusades, had fired the old spirit of Norse adventure left by the Danes, and England shared the general madness of the time. As a result for the treasure spent and blood spilled in Palestine, she received a few architectural devices and the science of Heraldry. But to Europe, the benefits were incalculable. The barons were impoverished, their great estates mortgaged to thrifty burghers, who extorted from their poverty charters of freedom, which unlocked the fetters and broke the spell of the dark ages.

Richard the Lion-Hearted died as he had lived, not as a king, but as a romantic adventurer. He was shot by an arrow while trying to secure fabulous hidden treasure in France, with which to continue his wars in Palestine.

[Sidenote: John, 1199-1216. Prince Arthur's Murder, 1203]

His brother John, in 1199, ascended the throne. His name has come down as a type of baseness, cruelty, and treachery. His brother Geoffrey had married Constance of Brittany, and their son Arthur, named after the Keltic hero, had been urged as a rival claimant for the English throne. Shakespeare has not exaggerated the cruel fate of this boy, whose monstrous uncle really purposed having his eyes burnt out, being sure that if he were blind he would no longer be eligible for king. But death is surer even than blindness, and Hubert, his merciful protector from one fate, was powerless to avert the other. Some one was found with "heart as hard as hammered iron, " who put an end to the young life (1203) at the Castle of Rouen.

But the King of England, was vassal to the King of France, and Philip summoned John to account to him for this deed. When John refused to appear, the French provinces were torn from him. In 1204 he saw an Empire stretching from the English Channel to the Pyrenees vanish from his grasp, and was at one blow reduced to the realm of England.

When we see on the map, England as she was in that day, sprawling in unwieldy fashion over the western half of France, we realize how much stronger she has been on "that snug little island, that right little, tight little island, " and we can see that John's wickedness helped her to be invincible.

The destinies of England in fact rested with her worst king. His tyranny, brutality, and disregard of his subjects' rights, induced a crisis which laid the corner-stone of England's future, and buttressed her liberties for all time.

[Sidenote: Magna Charta, 1215]

At a similar crisis in France, two centuries later, the king (Charles VII.) made common cause with the people against the barons or dukes. In England, in the 13th Century, the barons and people were drawn together against the King. They framed a Charter, its provisions securing protection and justice to every freeman in England. On Easter Day, 1215, the barons, attended by two thousand armed knights, met the King near Oxford, and demanded his signature to the paper. John was awed, and asked them to name a day and place. "Let the day be the 15th of June, and the place Runnymede, " was the reply.

A brown, shrivelled piece of parchment in the British Museum to-day, attests to the keeping of this appointment. That old Oak at Runnymede, under whose spreading branches the name of John was affixed to the Magna Charta, was for centuries held the most sacred spot in England.

The Evolution of an Empire

It is an impressive picture we get of John, "the Lord's Anointed, " when this scene was over, in a burst of rage rolling on the floor, biting straw, and gnawing a stick! "They have placed twenty-five kings over me, " he shouted in a fury; meaning the twenty-five barons who were entrusted with the duty of seeing that the provisions of the Charter were fulfilled.

Whether his death, one year later (1216), was the result of vexation of spirit or surfeit of peaches and cider, or poison, history does not positively say. But England shed no tears for the King to whom she owes her liberties in the Magna Charta.

CHAPTER IV.

[Sidenote: Henry III., 1216-1272]

For the succeeding 56 years John's son, Henry III., was King of England. While this vain, irresolute, ostentatious king was extorting money for his ambitious designs and extravagant pleasures, and struggling to get back the pledges given in the Great Charter, new and higher forces, to which he gave no heed, were at work in his kingdom.

Paris at this time was the centre of a great intellectual revival, brought about by the Crusades. We have seen that through the despised Jew, at the time of the Conquest, a higher civilization was brought into England. Along with his hoarded gold came knowledge and culture, which he had obtained from the Saracen. Now, these germs had been revived by direct contact with the sources of ancient knowledge in the East during the Crusades; and while the long mental torpor of Europe was rolling away like mist before the rising sun, England felt the warmth of the same quickening rays, and Oxford took on a new life.

[Sidenote: Oxford in the Thirteenth Century.]

It was not the stately Oxford of to-day, but a rabble of roystering, revelling youths, English, Welsh, and Scotch, who fiercely fought out their fathers' feuds.

They were a turbulent mob, who gave advance opinion, as it were, upon every ecclesiastical or political measure, by fighting it out on the streets of their town, so that an outbreak at Oxford became a sort of prelude to every great political movement.

Impossible as it seems, intellectual life grew and expanded in this tumultuous atmosphere; and while the democratic spirit of the University threatened the king, its spirit of free intellectual inquiry shook the Church.

The revival of classical learning, bringing streams of thought from old Greek and Latin fountains, caused a sudden expansion. It was like the discovery of an unsuspected and greater world, with a body of new truth, which threw the old into contemptuous disuse. A spirit of doubt, scepticism, and denial, was engendered. They comprehended now why Abelard had claimed the "supremacy of reason over faith, " and why Italian poets smiled at dreams of "immortality. " Then, too, the new culture compelled respect for infidel and for Jew. Was it not from their impious hands, that this new knowledge of the physical universe had been received?

[Sidenote: Roger Bacon Writes Opus Majus.]

Roger Bacon drank deeply from these fountains, new and old, and struggled like a giant to illumine the darkness of his time, by systematizing all existing knowledge. His "Opus Majus" was intended to bring these riches to the unlearned. But he died uncomprehended, and it was reserved for later ages to give recognition to his stupendous work, wrought in the twilight out of dimly comprehended truth.

Pursued by the dream of recovering the French Empire, lost by his father, and of retracting the promises given in the Charter, Henry III. spent his entire reign in conflict with the barons and the people, who were closely drawn together by the common danger and rallied to the defence of their liberties under the leadership of Simon de Montfort.

[Sidenote: Beginnings of House of Commons, 1265. First true Parliament, 1295. Edward I., 1272-1307]

It was at the town of Oxford that the great council of barons and bishops held its meetings. This council, which had long been called "Parliament" (from *parler*), in the year 1265 became for the first time a representative body, when Simon de Montfort summoned not alone the lords and bishops—but two citizens from every city, and two burghers from every borough. A Rubicon was passed when the merchant, and the shopkeeper, sat for the first time with the noble and the bishops in the great council. It was thirty years before the change was fully effected, it being in the year 1295 (just 600 years ago now) that the first true Parliament met. But the "House of Lords" and the germ of the "House of Commons, " existed in this assembly at Oxford in 1265, and a government "of the people, for the people, by the people, " had commenced.

The Evolution of an Empire

Edward I., the son and successor of Henry III., not only graciously confirmed the Great Charter, but added to its privileges. His expulsion of the Jews, is the one dark blot on his reign.

[Sidenote: North Wales Conquered, 1213. Conquest of Scotland, 1296.]

He conquered North Wales, the stronghold where those Keltic Britons, the Welsh, had always maintained a separate existence; and as a recompense for their wounded feelings bestowed upon the heir to the throne, the title *"Prince of Wales."*

Westminster Abbey was completed at this time and began to be the resting-place for England's illustrious dead. The invention of gunpowder, which was to make iron-clad knights a romantic tradition, also belongs to this period, which saw too, the conquest of Scotland; and the magic stone supposed to have been Jacob's pillow at Bethel, and which was the Scottish talisman, was carried to Westminster Abbey and built into a coronation-chair, which has been used at the crowning of every English sovereign since that time.

Scottish liberties were not so sacrificed by this conquest as had been the Irish. The Scots would not be slaves, nor would they stay conquered without many a struggle.

[Sidenote: Robert Bruce, Bannockburn, 1314. Edward II., King 1307-1327. Edward III., 1327-1377.]

Robert Bruce led a great rebellion, which extended into the succeeding reign, and Bruce's name was covered with glory by his great victory at Bannockburn (1314).

We need not linger over the twenty years during which Edward II., by his private infamies, so exasperated his wife and son that they brought about his deposition, which was followed soon after by his murder; and then by a disgraceful regency, during which the Queen's favorite, Mortimer, was virtually king. But King Edward III. commenced to rule with a strong hand. As soon as he was eighteen years old he summoned the Parliament. Mortimer was hanged at Tyburn, and his queen-mother was immured for life.

We have turned our backs upon Old England. The England of a representative Parliament and a House of Commons, of ideals derived from a wider knowledge, the England of a Westminster Abbey, and gunpowder, and cloth-weaving, is the England we all know to-day. Vicious kings and greed of territory, and lust of power, will keep the road from being a smooth one. but it leads direct to the England of Victoria; and 1895 was roughly outlined in 1327, when Edward III. grasped the helm with the decision of a master.

[Sidenote: Battle of Crecy, 1346]

After completing the subjection of Scotland he invaded France, —the pretext of resisting her designs upon the Netherlands, being merely a cover for his own thirst for territory and conquest. The victory over the French at Crecy, 1346, (and later of Poitiers,) covered the warlike king and his son, Edward the "Black Prince, " with imperishable renown. Small cannon were first used at that battle. The knights and the archers laughed at the little toy, but found it useful in frightening the enemies' horses.

Edward III. covered England with a mantle of military glory, for which she had to pay dearly later. He elevated the kingship to a more dazzling height, for which there have also been some expensive reckonings since. He introduced a new and higher dignity into nobility by the title of Duke, which he bestowed upon his sons; the great landholders or barons, having until that time constituted a body in which all were peers. He has been the idol of heroic England. But he awoke the dream of French conquest, and bequeathed to his successors a fatal war, which lasted for 100 years.

The "Black Prince" died, and the "Black Death, " a fearful pestilence, desolated a land already decimated by protracted wars. The valiant old King, after a life of brilliant triumphs, carried a sad and broken heart to the grave, and Richard II., son of the heroic Prince Edward, was king.

[Sidenote: Richard II., 1377-1399. Wat Tyler's Rebellion 1381.]

This last of the Plantagenets had need of great strength and wisdom to cope with the forces stirring at that time in his kingdom, and was singularly deficient in both. The costly conquests of his grandfather, were a troublesome legacy to his feeble grandson. Enormous taxes unjustly levied to pay for past glories, do not improve the temper of a people. A shifting of the burden from one class to another arrayed all in antagonisms against each other, and finally, when the burden

The Evolution of an Empire

fell upon the lowest order, as it is apt to do, they rose in fierce rebellion under the leadership of Wat Tyler, a blacksmith (1381).

Concessions were granted and quiet restored, but the people had learned a new way of throwing off injustice. There began to be a new sentiment in the air. Men were asking why the few should dress in velvet and the many in rags. It was the first revolt against the tyranny of wealth, when people were heard on the streets singing the couplet

> "When Adam delved and Eve span,
> Who was then the gentleman? "

As in the times of the early Saxon kings, the cause breeding destruction was the widening distance between the king and the people. In those earlier times the people unresistingly lapsed into decadence, but the Anglo-Saxon had learned much since then, and it was not so safe to degrade him and trample on his rights.

[Sidenote: John Wickliffe, 1324-1384.]

Then, too, John Wickliffe had been telling some very plain truths to the people about the Church of Rome, and there was developing a sentiment which made Pope and Clergy tremble. There was a spirit of inquiry, having its centre at Oxford, looking into the title-deeds of the great ecclesiastical despotism. Wickliffe heretically claimed that the Bible was the one ground of faith, and he added to his heresy by translating that Book into simple Saxon English, that men might learn for themselves what was Christ's message to man.

Luther's protest in the 16th Century was but the echo of Wickliffe's in the 14th, —against the tyranny of a Church from which all spiritual life had departed, and which in its decay tightened its grasp upon the very things which its founder put "behind Him" in the temptation on the mountain, and aimed at becoming a temporal despotism.

Closely intermingled with these struggles was going on another, unobserved at the time. Three languages held sway in England— Latin in the Church, French in polite society, and English among the people. Chaucer's genius selected the language of the people for its expression, as also of course, did Wickliffe in his translation of the Bible. French and Latin were dethroned, and the "King's English" became the language of the literature and speech of the English nation.

[Sidenote: 1399 Deposition of Richard II. House of Plantagenet ends 1399.]

He would have been a wise and great King who could have comprehended and controlled all the various forces at work at this time. Richard II. was neither. This seething, tumbling mass of popular discontents was besides only the groundwork for the personal strifes and ambitions which raged about the throne. The wretched King, embroiled with every class and every party, was pronounced by Parliament unfit to reign, the same body which deposed him, giving the crown to his cousin Henry of Lancaster (1399), and the reign of the Plantagenets was ended.

CHAPTER V.

[Sidenote: House of Lancaster, 1399-1461. Henry IV., 1399-1413.]

The new king did not inherit the throne; he was *elected* to it. He was an arbitrary creation of Parliament. The Duke of Lancaster, Henry's father (John of Gaunt), was only a younger son of Edward III. According to the strict rules of hereditary succession, there were two others with claims superior to Henry's. Richard Duke of York, his cousin, claimed a double descent from the Duke Clarence and also from the Duke of York, both sons of Edward III.

This led later to the dreariest chapter in English history, "the Wars of the Roses. "

It is an indication of the enormous increase in the strength of Parliament, that such an exercise of power, the creating of a king, was possible. Haughty, arrogant kings bowed submissively to its will. Henry could not make laws nor impose taxes without first summoning Parliament and obtaining his subjects' consent. But corrupting influences were at work which were destined to cheat England out of her liberties for many a year.

The impoverishment of the country to pay for war and royal extravagances, had awakened a troublesome spirit in the House of Commons. Cruelty to heretics also, and oppressive enactments were fought and defeated in this body. The King, clergy, and nobles, were drawing closer together and farther away from the people, and were devising ways of stifling their will.

If the King might not resist the will of Parliament, he could fill it with men who would not resist his; so, by a system of bribery and force in the boroughs, the House of Commons had injected into it enough of the right sort to carry obnoxious measures. This was only one of the ways in which the dearly bought liberties were being defeated.

Henry IV., the first Lancastrian king, lighted the fires of persecution in England. The infamous "Statute of Heresy" was passed 1401. Its first victim was a priest who was thrown to the flames for denying the doctrine of transubstantiation.

The Evolution of an Empire

Wickliffe had left to the people not a party, but a sentiment. The "Lollards, " as they were called, were not an organization, but rather a pervading atmosphere of revolt, which naturally combined with the social discontent of the time, and there came to be more of hate than love in the movement, which was at its foundation a revolt against inequality of condition. As in all such movements, much that was vicious and unwise in time mingled with it, tending to give some excuse for its repression. The discarding of an old faith, unless at once replaced by a new one, is a time fraught with many dangers to Society and State.

[Sidenote: Henry V. 1413-1422]

Such were some of the forces at work for fourteen brief years while Henry IV. wore the coveted crown, and while his son, the roystering "Prince Hal, " in the new character of King (Henry V.) lived out his brief nine years of glory and conquest.

[Sidenote: Agincourt, 1415]

France, with an insane King, vicious Queen Regent, and torn by the dissensions of ambitious Dukes, had reached her hour of greatest weakness, when Henry V. swept down upon her with his archers, and broke her spirit by his splendid victory at Agincourt; then married her Princess Katharine, and was proclaimed Regent of France. The rough wooing of his French bride, immortalized by Shakespeare, throws a glamour of romance over the time.

But an all-subduing King cut short Henry's triumphs. He was stricken and died (1422), leaving an infant son nine months old, who bore the weight of the new title, "King of England and France, " while Henry's brother, the Duke of Bedford, reigned as Regent.

[Sidenote: Joan of Arc. Battle of Orleans 1429.]

Then it was, that by a mysterious inspiration, Joan of Arc, a child and a peasant, led the French army to the besieged City of Orleans, and the crucial battle was won.

Charles VII. was King. The English were driven out of France, and the Hundred Years' War ended in defeat (1453). England had lost Aquitaine, which for two hundred years (since Henry II.) had been hers, and had not a foot of ground on Norman soil.

The Evolution of an Empire

The long shadow cast by Edward III upon England was deepening. A ruinous war had drained her resources and arrested her liberties; and now the odium of defeat made the burdens it imposed intolerable. The temper of every class was strained to the danger point. The wretched government was held responsible, followed, as usual, by impeachments, murders, and impotent outbursts of fury.

[Sidenote: Jack Cade's Insurrection, 1450]

While, owing to social processes long at work, feudalism was in fact a ruin, a mere empty shell, it still seemed powerful as ever; just as an oak, long after its roots are dead, will still carry aloft a waving mass of green leafage. The great Earl of Warwick when he went to Parliament was still followed by 600 liveried retainers. But when Jack Cade led 20,000 men in rebellion at the close of the French war, they were not the serfs and villeinage of other times, but farmers and laborers, who, when they demanded a more economical expenditure of royal revenue, freedom at elections, and the removal of restrictions on their dress and living, knew their rights, and were not going to give them up without a struggle.

But the madness of personal ambition was going to work deeper ruin and more complete wreck of England's fortunes. We have seen that by the interposition of Parliament, the House of Lancaster had been placed on the throne contrary to the tradition which gave the succession to the oldest branch, which Richard, the Duke of York, claimed to represent; his claim strengthened by a double descent from Edward III. through his two sons, Lionel and Edward.

[Sidenote: Wars of the Roses 1455-1485]

For twenty-one years, (1450-1471) these wars of the descendants of Edward III. were engaged in the most savage war, for purely selfish and personal ends, with not one noble or chivalric element to redeem the disgraceful exhibition of human nature at its worst. Murders, executions, treacheries, adorn a network of intrigue and villany, which was enough to have made the "White" and the "Red Rose" forever hateful to English eyes.

The great Earl of Warwick led the White Rose of York to victory, sending the Lancastrian King to the tower, his wife and child fugitives from the Kingdom, and proclaimed Edward, (son of

The Evolution of an Empire

Richard Duke of York, the original claimant, who had been slain in the conflict), King of England.

[Sidenote: Death of Henry VI. House of York, 1461-1485.]

Then, with an unscrupulousness worthy of the time and the cause, Warwick opened communication with the fugitive Queen, offering her his services, betrothed his daughter to the young Edward, Prince of Wales, took up the red Lancastrian rose from the dust of defeat, — brought the captive he had sent to the tower back to his throne — only to see him once more dragged down again by the Yorkists — and for the last time returned to captivity; leaving his wife a prisoner and his young son dead at Tewksbury, stabbed by Yorkist lords. Henry VI. died in the Tower, "mysteriously, " as did all the deposed and imprisoned Kings; Warwick was slain in battle, and with Edward IV, the reign of the House of York commenced.

Such in brief is the story of the *"Wars of the Roses"* and of the Earl of Warwick, the *"King Maker."*

[Sidenote: Edward IV., 1471-1483.]

At the close of the Wars of the Roses, feudalism was a ruin. The oak with its dead roots had been prostrated by the storm. The imposing system had wrought its own destruction. Eighty Princes of the blood royal had perished, and more than half of the Nobility had died on the field or the scaffold, or were fugitives in foreign lands. The great Duke of Exeter, brother-in-law to a King, was seen barefoot begging bread from door to door.

By the confiscation of one-fifth of the landed estate of the Kingdom, vast wealth poured into the King's treasury. He had no need now to summon Parliament to vote him supplies. The clergy, rendered feeble and lifeless from decline in spiritual enthusiasm, and by its blind hostility to the intellectual movement of the time, crept closer to the throne, while Parliament, with its partially disfranchised House of Commons, was so rarely summoned that it almost ceased to exist. In the midst of the general wreck, the Kingship towered in solitary greatness.

Edward IV. was absolute sovereign. He had no one to fear, unless it was his intriguing brother Richard, Duke of Gloucester, who, during the twenty-three years of Edward's reign, was undoubtedly carefully

The Evolution of an Empire

planning the bloodstained steps by which he himself should reach the throne.

Acute in intelligence, distorted in form and in character, this Richard was a monster of iniquity. The hapless boy left heir to the throne upon the death of Edward IV., his father, was placed under the guardianship of his misshapen uncle, who until the majority of the young King, Edward V., was to reign under the title of Protector.

[Sidenote: Richard III., 1483-1485. Death of the Princes in the Tower.]

How this "Protector" protected his nephews all know. The two boys (Edward V. and Richard, Duke of York) were carried to the Tower. The world has been reluctant to believe that they were really smothered, as has been said; but the finding, nearly two hundred years later, of the skeletons of two children which had been buried or concealed at the foot of the stairs leading to their place of confinement, seems to confirm it beyond a doubt.

[Sidenote: Bosworth Field. House of Tudor, 1485-1603. Henry VII., 1485-1509.]

Retribution came swiftly. Two years later Richard fell at the battle of Bosworth Field, and the crown won by numberless crimes, rolled under a hawthorn bush. It was picked up and placed upon a worthier head.

Henry Tudor, an offshoot of the House of Lancaster, was proclaimed King Henry VII., and his marriage with Princess Elizabeth of York (sister of the princes murdered in the Tower) forever blended the White and the Red Rose in peaceful union.

[Sidenote: Printing Introduced into England.]

During all this time, while Kings came and Kings went, the people viewed these changes from afar. But if they had no longer any share in the government, a great expansion was going on in their inner life. Caxton had set up his printing press, and the "art preservative of all arts, " was bringing streams of new knowledge into thousands of homes. Copernicus had discovered a new Heaven, and Columbus a new Earth. The sun no longer circled around the Earth, nor was the Earth a flat plain. There was a revival of classic learning at Oxford, and Erasmus, the great preacher, was founding schools and preparing the minds of the people for the impending change, which was soon to be wrought by that Monk in Germany, whose soul was at this time beginning to be stirred to its mighty effort at reform.

CHAPTER VI.

[Sidenote: Henry VIII., 1509-1517]

When in the year 1509 a handsome youth of eighteen came to the throne, the hopes of England ran high. His intelligence, his frank, genial manners, his sympathy with the "new learning, " won all classes. Erasmus in his hopes of purifying the Church, and Sir Thomas More in his "Utopian" dreams for politics and society, felt that a friend had come to the throne in the young Henry VIII.

Spain had become great through a union of the rival Kingdoms Castile and Aragon; so a marriage with the Princess Katharine, daughter of Ferdinand and Isabella, had been arranged for the young Prince Henry, who had quietly accepted for his Queen his brother's widow, six years his senior.

France under Francis I. had risen into a state no less imposing than Spain, and Henry began to be stirred with an ambition to take part in the drama of events going on upon the greater stage, across the Channel. The old dream of French conquest returned. Francis I. and Charles V. of Germany had commenced their struggle for supremacy in Europe. Henry's ambition was fostered by their vying with each other to secure his friendship. He was soon launched in a deep game of diplomacy, in which three intriguing Sovereigns were striving each to outwit the others.

What Henry lacked in experience and craft was supplied by his Chancellor Wolsey, whose private and personal ambition to reach the Papal Chair was dexterously mingled with the royal game. The game was dazzling and absorbing, but it was unexpectedly interrupted; and the golden dreams of Erasmus and More, of a slow and orderly development in England through an expanding intelligence, were rudely shaken.

Martin Luther audaciously nailed on the door of the Church at Wittenberg a protest against the selling of papal indulgences, and the pent-up hopes, griefs and despair of centuries burst into a storm which shook Europe to its centre.

[Sidenote: Reformation, 1517]

The Evolution of an Empire

Since England had joined in the great game of European politics, she had advanced from being a third-rate power to the front rank among nations; so it was with great satisfaction that Catholic Europe heard Henry VIII. denounce the new Reformation, which had swiftly assumed alarming proportions.

[Sidenote: Marriage with Anne Boleyn, 1533.]

But a woman's eyes were to change all this. As Henry looked into the fair face of Anne Boleyn, his conscience began to be stirred over his marriage with his brother's widow, Katharine. He confided his scruples to Wolsey, who promised to use his efforts with the Pope to secure a divorce from Katharine. But this lady was niece to Charles V., the great Champion of the Church in its fight with Protestantism. It would never do to alienate him. So the divorce was refused.

Henry VIII. was not as flexible and amiable now as the youth of eighteen had been. He defied the Pope, married Anne (1533), and sent his Minister into disgrace for not serving him more effectually. "There was the weight which pulled me down, " said Wolsey of Anne, and death from a broken heart mercifully saved the old man from the scaffold he would certainly have reached.

The legion of demons which had been slumbering in the King were awakened. He would break no law, but he would bend the law to his will. He commanded a trembling Parliament to pass an act sustaining his marriage with Anne. Another permitting him to name his successor, and then another—making him *supreme head of the Church in England*. The Pope was forever dethroned in his Kingdom, and Protestantism had achieved a bloodstained victory.

[Sidenote: His Supremacy. Henry a Protestant. Anne Boleyn's Death, 1536.]

Henry alone could judge what was orthodoxy and what heresy; but to disagree with *him*, was death. Traitor and heretic went to the scaffold in the same hurdle; the Catholic who denied the King's supremacy riding side by side with the Protestant who denied transubstantiation. The Protestantism of this great convert was political, not religious; he despised the doctrines of Lutheranism, and it was dangerous to believe too much and equally dangerous to believe too little. Heads dropped like leaves in the forest, and in three years the Queen who had overturned England and almost Europe, was herself carried to the scaffold (1536).

It was in truth a "Reign of Terror" by an absolutism standing upon the ruin of every rival. The power of the Barons had gone; the Clergy were panic-stricken, and Parliament was a servant, which arose and bowed humbly to his vacant throne at mention of his name! A member for whom he had sent knelt trembling one day before him. "Get my bill passed to-morrow, my little man, " said the King, "or to-morrow, this head of yours will be off. " The next day the bill passed, and millions of Church property was confiscated, to be thrown away in gambling, or to enrich the adherents of the King.

Thomas Cromwell, who had succeeded to Wolsey's vacant place, was his efficient instrument. This student of Machiavelli's "Prince, " without passion or hate, pity or regret, marked men for destruction, as a woodman does tall trees, the highest and proudest names in the Kingdom being set down in his little notebook under the head of either "Heresy" or "Treason. " Sir Thomas More, one of the wisest and best of men, would not say he thought the marriage with Katharine had been unlawful, and paid his head as the price of his fearless honesty.

Jane Seymour, whom Henry married the day after Anne Boleyn's execution, died within a year at the birth of a son (Edward VI.). In 1540 Cromwell arranged another union with the plainest woman in Europe, Anne of Cleves; which proved so distasteful to Henry that he speedily divorced her, and in resentment at Cromwell's having entrapped him, by a flattering portrait drawn by Holbein, the Minister came under his displeasure, which at that time meant death. He was beheaded in 1540, and in that same year occurred the King's marriage with Katharine Howard, who one year later met same fate as Anne Boleyn.

[Sidenote: Katherine Howard's Death 1541. Death of Henry VIII., 1547.]

Katharine Parr, the fifth and last wife, and an ardent Protestant and reformer, also narrowly escaped, and would undoubtedly at last have gone to the block. But Henry, who at fifty-six was infirm and wrecked in health, died in the year 1547, the signing of death-warrants being his occupation to the very end.

The Evolution of an Empire

Whatever his motive, Henry VIII. had in making her Protestant, placed England firmly in the line of the world's highest progress; and strange to say, that Kingdom is most indebted to two of her worst Kings.

[Sidenote: Edward VI 1547-1555. Lady Jane Grey's Death, 1553.]

The crown passed to the son of Jane Seymour, Edward VI., a feeble boy of sixteen, and upon his death six years later (1553), by the King's will to Lady Jane Grey, descendant of his sister Mary. This gentle girl of seventeen, sensitive and thoughtful, a devout reformer, who read Greek and Hebrew and wrote Latin poetry, is a pathetic figure in history, where we see her, the unwilling wearer of a crown for ten days, and then with her young husband hurried to that fatal Tower, and to death; a brief touching interlude before the crowning of Mary, daughter of Henry and Katharine of Aragon.

Henry VIII. stoutly adhered to Protestantism, and preferred that the succession should pass out of his own family, rather than into Catholic dominion again. Hence his naming of Jane Grey instead of his own daughter Mary, in case of the death of his delicate son Edward.

But Henry was no longer there to stem the tide of Catholic sentiment. Lady Jane Grey was hurried to the block, and the Catholic Mary to the throne.

[Sidenote: Mary 1553-1558. Calais Lost, 1558]

Her marriage with Philip II. of Spain quickly overthrew the work of her father. Unlike Henry VIII., Mary was impelled by deep conviction. She persecuted to save from what she believed eternal death. Her cruelty was prompted by sincere fanaticism, mingled with the desire to please the Catholic Philip, whose love she craved and could not win. Disappointed in his aim to reign jointly with her, as he had hoped, he withdrew to Spain. Unlovely and unloved, she is almost an object of pity, as with dungeon, rack and fagot she strives to restore the Religion she loves, and to win the husband she adores. But Philip remained obdurately in Spain, and while she was lighting up all England with a blaze of martyrs, Calais, the last English possession in France, was lost. Mary died amid crushing disappointments public and personal, after reigning five years (1553-1558).

CHAPTER VII.

[Sidenote: Elizabeth, 1558-1603.]

Elizabeth, daughter of Henry and a disgraced and decapitated Queen, wore the crown of England. If heredity had been as much talked of then as now, England might have feared the child of a faithless wife, and a remorseless, bloodthirsty King. But while Mary, daughter of Katharine, the most pious and best of mothers, had left only a great blood-spot upon the page of History, Elizabeth's reign was to be the most wise, prosperous and great, the Kingdom had ever known. In her complex character there was the imperiousness, audacity and unscrupulousness of her father, the voluptuous pleasure-loving nature of her mother, and mingled with both, qualities which came from neither. She was a tyrant, held in check by a singular caution, with an instinctive perception of the presence of danger, to which her purposes always instantly bent.

The authority vested in her was as absolute as her father's, but while her imperious temper sacrificed individuals without mercy, she ardently desired the welfare of her Kingdom, which she ruled with extraordinary moderation and a political sagacity almost without parallel, softening, but not abandoning, one of her father's usurpations.

She was a Protestant without any enthusiasm for the religion she intended to restore in England, and prayed to the Virgin in her own private Chapel, while she was undoing the work of her Catholic sister Mary. The obsequious apologies to the Pope were withdrawn, but the Reformation she was going to espouse, was not the fiery one being fought for in Germany and France. It was mild, moderate, and like her father's, more political than religious. The point she made was that there must be religious uniformity, and conformity to the Established Church of England—with its new "Articles, " which as she often said, "left *opinion* free. "

It was in fact a softened reproduction of her terrible father's attitude. The Church, (called an "Episcopacy, " on account of the jurisdiction of its Bishops,) was Protestant in doctrine, with gentle leaning toward Catholicism in externals, held still firmly by the "Act of Supremacy" in the controlling hand of the Sovereign. Above all else desiring peace and prosperity for England, the keynote of Elizabeth's policy in Church and in State was conciliation and compromise. So the Church of England was to a great extent a compromise, retaining as much as the people would bear of external form and ritual, for the sake of reconciling Catholic England.

The large element to whom this was offensive was reinforced by returning refugees who brought with them the stern doctrines of Calvin; and they finally separated themselves altogether from a Church in which so much of Papacy still lingered, to establish one upon simpler and purer foundation; hence they were called "Puritans, " and "Nonconformists, " and were persecuted for violation of the "Act of Supremacy. "

The masculine side of Elizabeth's character was fully balanced by her feminine foibles. Her vanity was inordinate. Her love of adulation and passion for display, her caprice, duplicity, and her reckless love-affairs, form a strange background for the calm, determined, masterly statesmanship under which her Kingdom expanded.

The subject of her marriage was a momentous one. There were plenty of aspirants for the honor. Her brother-in-law Philip, since the abdication of Charles V., his father, was a mighty King, ruler over Spain and the Netherlands, and was at the head of Catholic Europe. He saw in this vain, silly young Queen of England an easy prey. By marrying her he could bring England back to the fold, as he had done with her sister Mary, and the Catholic cause would be invincible.

Elizabeth was a coquette, without the personal charm supposed to belong to that dangerous part of humanity. She toyed with an offer of marriage as does a cat with a mouse. She had never intended to marry Philip, but she kept him waiting so long for her decision, and so exasperated him with her caprice, that he exclaimed at last, "That girl has ten thousand devils in her. " He little thought, that beneath that surface of folly there was a nature hard as steel, and a calm, clear, cool intelligence, for which his own would be no match, and which would one day hold in check the diplomacy of the "Escurial" and outwit that of Europe. She adored the culture brought by the "new learning; " delighted in the society of Sir Philip Sidney, who reflected all that was best in England of that day; talked of poetry with Spenser; discussed philosophy with Bruno; read Greek tragedies and Latin orations in the original; could converse in French and Italian, and was besides proficient in another language, —the language of the fishwife, —which she used with startling effect with her lords and ministers when her temper was aroused, and swore like a trooper if occasion required.

But whatever else she was doing she never ceased to study the new England she was ruling. She felt, though did not understand, the expansion which was going on in the spirit of the people; but instinctively realized the necessity for changes and modifications in her Government, when the temper of the nation seemed to require it.

It was enormous common-sense and tact which converted Elizabeth into a liberal Sovereign. Her instincts were despotic. When she bowed instantly to the will of the Commons, almost apologizing for seeming to resist it, it was not because she sympathized with liberal sentiments, but because of her profound political instincts, which taught her the danger of alienating that class upon which the greatness of her Kingdom rested. She realized the truth forgotten by some of her successors, that the Sovereign and the middle class *must be friends*. She might resist and insult her lords and ministers, send great Earls and favorites ruthlessly to the block, but no slightest cloud must come between her and her "dear Commons" and people. This it was which made Spenser's adulation in the "Faerie Queen" but an expression of the intense loyalty of her meanest subject.

Perhaps it was because she remembered that the whole fabric of the Church rested upon Parliamentary enactment, and that she herself was Queen of England by Parliamentary sanction, that she viewed so complacently the growing power of that body in dealing more and more with matters supposed to belong exclusively to the Crown, as for instance in the struggle made by the Commons to suppress monopolies in trade, granted by royal prerogative. At the first she angrily resisted the measure. But finding the strength of the popular sentiment, she gracefully retreated, declaring, with royal scorn for truth, that "she had not before known of the existence of such an evil. "

In fact, lying, in her independent code of morals, was a virtue, and one to which she owed some of her most brilliant triumphs in diplomacy. And when the bald, unmitigated lie was at last found out, she felt not the slightest shame, but only amusement at the simplicity of those who had believed she was speaking the truth.

The Evolution of an Empire

[Sidenote: Massacre of St. Bartholomew's, 1572. East India Company Chartered, 1606. Colonization of Virginia.]

Her natural instincts, her thrift, and her love of peace inclined her to keep aloof from the struggle going on in Europe between Protestants and Catholics. But while the news of St. Bartholomew's Eve seemed to give her no thrill of horror, she still sent armies and money to aid the Huguenots in France, and to stem the persecutions of Philip in the Netherlands, and committed England fully to a cause for which she felt no enthusiasm. She encouraged every branch of industry, commerce, trade, fostered everything which would lead to prosperity. Listened to Raleigh's plans for colonization in America, permitting the New Colony to be called "Virginia" in her honor (the Virgin Queen). She chartered the "Merchant Company, " intended to absorb the new trade with the Indies (1600), and which has expanded into a British Empire in India.

But amid all this triumph, a sad and solitary woman sat on the throne of England. The only relation she had in the world was her cousin, Mary Stuart, who was plotting to undermine and supplant her.

The question of Elizabeth's legitimacy was an ever recurring one, and afforded a rallying point for malcontents, who asserted that her mother's marriage with Henry VIII. was invalidated by the refusal of the Pope to sanction the divorce. Mary Stuart, who stood next to Elizabeth in the succession, formed a centre from which a network of intrigue and conspiracy was always menacing the Queen's peace, if not her life, and her crown.

Scotland, since the extinction of the line of Bruce, had been ruled by the Stuart Kings. Torn by internal feuds between her clans, and by the incessant struggle against English encroachments, she had drawn into close friendship with France, which country used her for its own ends, in harassing England, so that the Scottish border was always a point of danger in every quarrel between French and English Kings.

[Sidenote: Flodden Field 1513. Birth of Mary Stuart 1542.]

In 1502 Henry VIII. had bestowed the hand of his sister Margaret upon James IV. of Scotland, and it seemed as if a peaceful union was at last secured with his Northern neighbor. But in the war with France which soon followed, James, the Scottish King, turned to his old ally. He was killed at "Flodden Field, " after suffering a crushing defeat. His successor, James V., had maried Mary Guise. Her family was the head and front of the ultra Catholic party in France, and her counsels probably influenced Edward to a continual hostility to the Protestant Henry, even though he was his uncle. The death of James in consequence of his defeat at "Solway Moss" occurred immediately after the birth of his daughter, Mary Stuart (1542).

This unhappy child at once became the centre of intriguing designs; Henry VIII. wishing to betroth the little Queen to his son, afterwards Edward VI., and thus forever unite the rival kingdoms. But the Guises made no compromises with Protestants! Mary Guise, who was now Regent of the realm, had no desire for a closer union with Protestant England, and very much desired a nearer alliance with her own France. Mary Stuart was betrothed to the Dauphin, son of Francis I., and was sent to the French Court to be prepared by Catharine de Medici (the Italian daughter-in-law of Francis I.) for her future exalted position.

[Sidenote: Mary Stuart Returns to England.]

In 1561, Mary returned to England. Her boy-husband had died after a reign of two years. She was nineteen years old, had wonderful beauty, rare intelligence, and power to charm like a siren. Her short life had been spent in the most corrupt and profligate of Courts, under the combined influence of Catharine de Medici, the worst woman in Europe, — and her two uncles of the House of Guise, who were little better. Political intrigues, plottings and crimes were in the very air she breathed from infancy. But she was an ardent and devout Catholic, and as such became the centre and the hope of what still remained of Catholic England.

Elizabeth would have bartered half her possessions for the one possession of beauty. That she was jealous of her fascinating rival there is little doubt, but that she was exasperated at her pretensions and at the audacious plottings against her life and throne is not strange. In fact we wonder that, with her imperious temper, she so long hesitated to strike the fatal blow.

Whether Mary committed the dark crimes attributed to her or not, we do not know. But we do know, that after the murder of her wretched husband, Lord Darnley, (her cousin, Henry Stuart), she quickly married the man to whom the deed was directly traced. Her

The Evolution of an Empire

marriage with Bothwell was her undoing. Scotland was so indignant at the act, that she took refuge in England, only to fall into Elizabeth's hands.

Mary Stuart had once audaciously said, "the reason her cousin did not marry was because she would not lose the power of compelling men to make love to her. " Perhaps the memory of this jest made it easier to sign the fatal paper in 1587.

[Sidenote: Mary Stuart's Death, 1587.]

When we read of Mary's irresistible charm, of her audacity, her cunning, her genius for diplomacy and statecraft, far exceeding Elizabeth's—when we read of all this and think of the blood of the Guises in her veins, and the precepts of Catharine de Medici in her heart, we realize what her usurpation would have meant for England, and feel that she was a menace to the State, and justly incurred her fate. Then again, when we hear of her gentle patience in her long captivity, her prayers and piety, and her sublime courage when she walked through the Hall at Fotheringay Castle, and laid her beautiful head on the block as on a pillow, we are melted to pity, and almost revolted at the act. It is difficult to be just, with such a lovely criminal, unless one is made of such stern stuff as was John Knox.

[Sidenote: James VI., King of Scotland. Defeat of Spanish Armada, 1597.] The son of Mary by Henry Stuart (Lord Darnley) was James VI. of Scotland. With his mother's death, all pretensions to the English throne were forever at rest. But Philip of Spain thought the time propitious for his own ambitious purposes, and sent an Armada (fleet) which approached the Coast in the form of a great Crescent, one mile across. The little English "seadogs, " not much larger than small pleasure yachts, were led by Sir Francis Drake. They worried the ponderous Spanish ships, and then, sending burning boats in amongst them, soon spoiled the pretty crescent. The fleet scattered along the Northern Coast, where it was overtaken by a frightful storm, and the winds and the waves completed the victory, almost annihilating the entire "Armada. "

[Sidenote: Francis Bacon.]

England was great and glorious. The revolution, religious, social and political, had ploughed and harrowed the surface which had been fertilized with the "New Learning, " and the harvest was rich. While all Europe was devastated by religious wars there arose in Protestant England such an era of peace and prosperity, with all the conditions of living so improved that the dreams of Sir Thomas More's "Utopia" seemed almost realized. The new culture was everywhere. England was garlanded with poetry, and lighted by genius, such as the world has not seen since, and may never see again. The name of Francis Bacon was sufficient to adorn an age, and that of Shakespeare alone, enough to illumine a century. Elizabeth did not create the glory of the "Elizabethan Age, " but she did create the peace and social order from which it sprang.

If this Queen ever loved any one it was the Earl of Leicester, the man who sent his lovely wife, Amy Robsart, to a cruel death in the delusive hope of marrying a Queen. We are unwilling to harbor the suspicion that she was accessory to this deed; and yet we cannot forget that she was the daughter of Henry VIII.! —and sometimes wonder if the memory of a crime as black as Mary's haunted her sad old age, when sated with pleasures and triumphs, lovers no more whispering adulation in her ears, and mirrors banished from her presence, she silently waited for the end.

She died in the year 1603, and succumbing to the irony of fate, named the son of Mary Stuart—James VI. of Scotland—her successor.

CHAPTER VIII.

[Sidenote: House of Stuart, 1603-1714.]

The House of Stuart had peacefully reached the long coveted throne of England in the person of a most unkingly King. Gross in appearance and vulgar in manners, James had none of the royal attributes of his mother. A great deal of knowledge had been crammed into a very small mind. Conceited, vain, pedantic, headstrong, he set to work with the confidence of ignorance to carry out his undigested views upon all subjects, reversing at almost every point the policy of his great predecessor. Where she with supreme tact had loosened the screws so that the great authority vested in her might not press too heavily upon the nation, he tightened them. Where she bowed her imperious will to that of the Commons, this puny tyrant insolently defied it, and swelling with sense of his own greatness, claimed, "Divine right" for Kingship and demanded that his people should say "the King can do no wrong, " "to question his authority is to question that of God. " If he ardently supported the Church of England, it was because he was its head. The Catholic who would have turned the Church authority over again to the Pope, and the "Puritans" who resisted the "Popish practices" of the Reformed Church of England, were equally hateful to him, for one and the same reason; they were each aiming to diminish *his* authority.

[Sidenote: First English Colony in New England]

When the Puritans brought to him a petition signed by 800 clergymen, praying that they be not compelled to wear the surplice, nor make the sign of the cross at baptism—he said they were "vipers, " and if they did not submit to the authority of the Bishops in such matters "they should be harried out of the land. " In the persecution implied by this threat, a large body of Puritans escaped to Holland with their families, and from thence came that band of heroic men and women on the "Mayflower, " landing at a point On the American Coast which they called "Plymouth" (1620). A few Englishmen had in 1607 settled in Jamestown, Virginia. These two colonies contained the germ of the future "United States of America. "

[Sidenote: "Gunpowder Plot, 1605. "]

The Evolution of an Empire

The persecution of the Catholics led to a plot to blow up Parliament House at a time when the King was present, thinking thus at one stroke to get rid of a usurping tyrant, and of a House of Commons which was daily becoming more and more infected with Puritanism. The discovery of this "Guy Fawkes gunpowder plot, " prevented its consummation, and immensely strengthened Puritan sentiment.

The keynote of Elizabeth's foreign policy had been hostility to Spain, that Catholic stronghold, and an unwavering adherence to Protestant Europe. James saw in that great and despotic government the most suitable friend for such a great King as himself. He proposed a marriage between his son Charles and the Infanta, daughter of the King of Spain, making abject promises of legislation in his Kingdom favorable to the Catholics; and when an indignant House of Commons protested against the marriage, they were insolently reprimanded for meddling with things which did not concern them, and were sent home, not to be recalled again until the King's necessities for money compelled him to summon them.

[Sidenote: Francis Bacon.]

During the early part of his reign the people seem to have been paralyzed and speechless before his audacious pretensions. Great courtiers were fawning at his feet listening to his pedantic wisdom, and humoring his theory of the "Divine right" of hereditary Kingship. And alas! —that we have to say it—Francis Bacon (his Chancellor), with intellect towering above his century, —was his obsequious servant and tool, uttering not one protest as one after another the liberties of the people were trampled upon!

But this Spanish marriage had aroused a spirit before which a wiser man than James would have trembled. He was standing midway between two scaffolds, that of his mother (1587), and his son (1649). Every blow he struck at the liberties of England cut deep into the foundation of his throne. And when he violated the law of the land by the imposition of taxes, without the sanction of his Parliament, he had "sowed the wind" and the "whirlwind, " which was to break on his son's head was inevitable. Popular indignation began to be manifest, and Puritan members of the Commons began to use language the import of which could not be mistaken. Bacon was disgraced; his crime, —while ostensibly the "taking of bribes, "—was in reality his being the servile tool of the King.

The Evolution of an Empire

[Sidenote: Translation of Bible. Great Britain.]

In reviewing the acts of this reign we see a foolish Sovereign ruled by an intriguing adventurer whom he created Duke of Buckingham. We see him foiled in his attempt to link the fate of England with that of Catholic Europe; —sacrificing Sir Walter Raleigh because he had given offense to Spain, the country whose friendship he most desired. We see numberless acts of folly, and but three which we can commend. James did authorize and promote the translation of the Bible which has been in use until today. He named his double Kingdom of England and Scotland "Great Britain. " These two acts, together with his death in 1625, meet with our entire approval.

[Sidenote: James' Death 1625. Charles I., 1625-1649.]

Charles I., son of James, was at least one thing which his father was not. He was a gentleman. Had it not been his misfortune to inherit a crown, his scholarly refinements and exquisite tastes, his irreproachable morals, and his rectitude in the personal relations of life, might have won him only esteem and honor. But these qualities belonged to Charles Stuart the gentleman. Charles the King was imperious, false, obstinate, blind to the conditions of his time, and ignorant of the nature of his people. Every step taken during his reign led him nearer to its fatal consummation.

No family in Europe ever grasped at power more unscrupulously than the Guises in France. They were cruel and remorseless in its pursuit. It was the warm southern blood of her mother which was Mary Stuart's ruin. She was a Guise, —and so was her son James I. —and so was Charles I., her grandson. There was despotism and tyranny in their blood. Their very natures made it impossible that they should comprehend the Anglo- Saxon ideal of civil liberty.

Who can tell what might have been the course of History, if England had been ruled by English Kings, which it has not been since the Conquest. With every royal marriage there is a fresh infusion of foreign blood drawn from fountains not always the purest, —until after centuries of such dilutions, the royal line has less of the Anglo-Saxon in it than any ancestral line in the Kingdom.

The odious Spanish marriage had been abandoned and Charles had married Henrietta, sister of Louis XIII. of France.

The Evolution of an Empire

[Sidenote: Archbishop Laud.]

The subject of religion was the burning one at that time. It soon became apparent that the new King's personal sympathies leaned as far as his position permitted toward Catholicism. The Church of England under its new Primate, Archbishop Laud, was being drawn farther away from Protestantism and closer to Papacy; while Laud in order to secure Royal protection advocated the absolutism of the King, saying that James in his theory of "Divine right" had been inspired by the Holy Ghost, thus turning religion into an engine of attack upon English liberties. Laud's ideal was a purified Catholicism—retaining auricular confession, prayers for the dead, the Real Presence in the Sacrament, genuflexions and crucifixes, all of which were odious to Puritans and Presbyterians. He had a bold, narrow mind, and recklessly threw himself against the religious instincts of the time. The same pulpit from which was read a proclamation ordering that the Sabbath be treated as a holiday, and not a Holy-day, was also used to tell the people that resistance to the King's will was "Eternal damnation."

This made the Puritans seem the defenders of the liberties of the country, and drew hosts of conservative Churchmen, such as Pym, to their side, although not at all in sympathy with a religious fanaticism which condemned innocent pleasures, and all the things which adorn life, as mere devices of the devil. Such were the means by which the line was at last sharply drawn. The Church of England and tyranny on one side, and Puritanism and liberty on the other.

But there was one thing which at this moment was of deeper interest to the King than religion. He wanted, —he must have, —money. *Religion* and *money* are the two things upon which the fate of nations has oftenest hung. These two dangerous factors were both present now, and they were going to make history very fast.

On account of a troublesome custom prevailing in his Kingdom, Charles must first summon his Parliament, and they must grant the needed supplies. His father had by the discovery of the theory of "Divine right," prepared the way to throw off these Parliamentary trammels. But that could only be reached by degrees. So Parliament was summoned. It had no objection to voting the needed subsidies, but, —the King must first promise certain reforms, political and religious, and—dismiss his odious Minister Buckingham.

The Evolution of an Empire

Charles, indignant at this outrage, dissolved the body, and appealed to the country for a loan. The same reply came from every quarter. "We will gladly lend the money, but it must be done through Parliament. " The King was thoroughly aroused. If the loan will not be voluntary, it must be forced. A tax was levied, fines and penalties for its resistance meted out by subservient judges.

[Sidenote: John Hampden, Petition of Right.]

John Hampden was one of the earliest victims. His means were ample, the sum was small, but his manhood was great. "Not one farthing, if it me cost my life, " was his reply as he sat in the prison at Gate House.

The supply did not meet the King's demand. Overwhelmed with debt and shame and rage, he was obliged again to resort to the hated means. Parliament was summoned. The Commons, with memory of recent outrages in their hearts, were more determined than before. The members drew up a *"Petition of Right, "* which was simply a reaffirmation of the inviolability of the rights of person, of property and of speech—a sort of second "Magna Charta. "

They resolutely and calmly faced their King, the "Petition" in one hand, the granted subsidies in the other. For a while he defied them; but the judges were whispering in his ear that the "Petition" would not be binding upon him, and Buckingham was urging him to yield. Perhaps it was Charles Stuart the gentleman who hesitated to receive money in return for solemn promises which he did not intend to keep! But Charles the King signed the paper, which seven judges out of twelve, in the highest court of the realm, were going to pronounce invalid because the King's power was beyond the reach of Parliament. It was inherent in him as King, and bestowed by God. *Any infringement upon his prerogative by Act of Parliament was void!*

With king so false, and with justice so polluted at its fountain, what hope was there for the people but in Revolution?

[Sidenote: Massachusetts Chartered, 1629]

From the tyranny of the Church under Laud, a way was opened when, in 1629, Charles granted a Charter to the Colony of Massachusetts. With a quiet, stern enthusiasm the hearts of men turned toward that refuge in America. Not men of broken fortunes, adventurers, and criminals, but owners of large landed estates, professional men, some of the best in the land, who abandoned home and comfort to face intolerable hardships. One wrote, "We are weaned from the delicate milk of our Mother England and do not mind these trials. " As the pressure increased under Laud, the stream toward the West increased in volume; so that in ten years 20,000 Englishmen had sought religious freedom across the sea, and had founded a Colony which, strange to say, —under the influence of an intense religious sentiment, —became itself a Theocracy and a new tyranny, although one sternly just and pure.

The dissolute, worthless Buckingham had been assassinated, and Charles had wept passionate tears over his dead body. But his place had been filled by one far better suited to the King's needs at a time when he had determined not again to recall Parliament, but to rule without it until resistance to his measures had ceased.

It was with no sinister purpose of establishing a despotism such as a stronger man might have harbored, that he made this resolve. What Charles wanted was simply the means of filling his exchequer; and if Parliament would not give him that except by a dicker for reforms, and humiliating pledges which he could not keep, why then he would find new ways of raising money without them. His father had done it before him, he had done it himself. With no Commons there to rate and insult him, it could be done without hindrance.

He was not grand enough, nor base enough, nor was he rich enough, to carry out any organized design upon the country. He simply wanted money, and had such blind confidence in Kingship, that any very serious resistance to his authority did not enter his dreams. It was the limitations of his intelligence which proved his ruin, his inability to comprehend a new condition in the spirit of his people. Elizabeth would have felt it, though she did not understand it, and would have loosened the screws, without regard for her personal preferences, and by doing it, so bound the people to her, that her policy would have been their policy. Charles was as wise as the engineer who would rivet down the safety-valves!

Sir Thomas Wentworth (Earl Strafford), who had taken the place of Buckingham, was an apostate from the party of liberty. Disappointed in becoming a leader in the Commons he had drawn gradually closer to the King, who now leaned upon him as the vine upon the oak.

The Evolution of an Empire

[Sidenote: Earl Strafford. The "Star Chamber."]

This man's ideal was to build up in England just such a despotism as Richelieu was building in France. The same imperious temper, the same invincible will and administrative genius, marked him as fitted for the work. While Charles was feebly scheming for revenue, he was laying large and comprehensive plans for a system of oppression, which should *yield* the revenue, —and for Arsenals and Forts—and a standing Army, and a rule of terror which should hold the nation in subjection while these things were preparing. He was clear-sighted enough to see that "absolutism" was not to be accomplished by a system of reasoning. He would not urge it as a dogma, but as a fact.

The "Star Chamber, " a tribunal for the trying of a certain class of offences, was brought to a state of fresh efficiency. Its punishments could be anything this side of death. A clergyman accused of speaking disrespectfully of Laud, is condemned to pay 5,000 pounds to the King, 300 pounds to the aggrieved Archbishop himself, one side of his nose is to be slit, one ear cut off, and one cheek branded. The next week this to be repeated on the other side, and then followed by imprisonment subject to pleasure of the Court. Another who has written a book considered seditious, has the same sentence carried out, only varied by imprisonment for life.

These were some of the embellishments of the system called "Thorough, " which was carried on by the two friends and confederates, Laud and Strafford, who were in their pleasant letters to each other all the time lamenting that the power of the "Star Chamber" was so limited, and judges so timid! Is it strange that the plantation in Massachusetts had fresh recruits?

But the more serious work was going on under Strafford's vigorous management. "Monopolies" were sold once more, with a fixed duty on profits added to the price of the original concession. Every article in use by the people was at last bought up by Monopolists, who were compelled to add to the price of these commodities, to compensate for the tax they must pay into the King's Treasury.

[Sidenote: Monoplies. Ship Money.]

"Ship Money" was a tax supposably for the building of a Navy, for which there was no accounting to the people, the amount and frequency of the levy being discretionary with the King. It was always possible and imminent, and was the most odious of all the methods adopted for wringing money from the nation, while resistance to it, as to all other such measures, was punished by the Star Chamber in such pleasant fashion as would please Strafford and Laud, whose creatures the judges were.

Hampden, as before, championed the rights of the people in his own person, going to prison and facing death, if it were necessary, rather than pay the amount of 20 shillings. But that the taxes were paid by the people is evident, for so successful was this scheme of revenue that many predicted the King would never again call a Parliament. What would be the need of a Parliament, if he did not require money? The Royalists were pleased, and the people were wisely patient, knowing that such a financial fabric must fall at the first breath of a storm, and then their time would come.

CHAPTER IX.

The storm came in the form of a war upon Scotland, to enforce the established Church, which it had cast out "root and branch" for the Presbyterianism which pleased it. The Loyalists were alarmed by rumors that Scotland was holding treasonable communication with her old ally, France; and after an interval of eleven years, a Parliament was summoned, which was destined to outlive the King.

[Sidenote: Long Parliament. Strafford Impeached.]

The Commons came together in stern temper, Pym standing promptly at the Bar of the House of Lords with Strafford's impeachment for High Treason. The great Earl's apologists among the Lords, his own ingenious and powerful pleadings, the King's entreaties and worthless promises, all were in vain.

The King saw the whole fabric of tyranny crumbling before his eyes. He was overawed and dared not refuse his signature to the fatal paper. It is said that as Strafford passed to the block, Laud, who was at the window of the room where he too was a prisoner, fainted as his old companion in cruelty stopped to say farewell to him.

There were a few moments of silence, then, —a wild exultant shout. "His head is off—His head is off. "

[Sidenote: Strafford's Death. Death of Laud.]

The execution of the Archbishop swiftly followed, then the abolition of the Star Chamber, and of the High Commission Court; then a bill was passed requiring that Parliament be summoned once in three years, and a law enacted *forbidding its dissolution except by its own consent.*

They were rapidly nearing the conception that Parliament does not exist by sanction of the King, but the King by sanction of Parliament.

What could be done with a King whom no promises could bind— who, while in the act of giving solemn pledges to Parliament in order to save Strafford, was perfidiously planning to overawe it by military force? The attempted arrest of Hampden, Pym, and three other leaders was part of this "Army Plot, " which made civil war inevitable. The trouble had resolved itself into a deadly conflict between King and Parliament. If he resorted to arms, so must they.

If Hampden stands out pre-eminent as the Champion who like a great Gladiator fought the battle of civil freedom, Pym is no less conspicious in having grasped the principles on which it must be fought. He saw that if either Crown or Parliament must go down, better for England that it should be the crown. He saw also, that the vital principle in Parliament lay in the House of Commons. If the King refused to act with them, it should be treated as an abdication, and Parliament must act without him, and if the Lords obstructed reform, then they must be told that the Commons must act alone, rather than let the Kingdom perish.

This was the theory upon which the future action was based. Revolutionary and without precedent it has since been accepted as the correct construction of English Constitutional principles.

[Sidenote: Oliver Cromwell.]

Better would it have been for Charles had he let the ship sail, which was to have borne Hampden and his Cousin, Oliver Cromwell, toward the "Valley of the Connecticut. " He recalled the man who was to be his evil genius when he gave that order. Cromwell could not so accurately have defined the constitutional right of his cause as Pym had done, nor make himself its adored head as was Hampden; but he had a more compelling genius than either. His figure stands up colossal and grim away above all others from the time he raised his praying, psalm-singing army, until the defeat of the King's forces at Naseby (1645), the flight of the King and his subsequent surrender.

It was at this time that Cromwell began to manifest as much ability as a political as he had done as a military leader. Hampden had fallen on the battlefield, Pym was dead, he was virtual head of the cause. Perhaps it needed just such a terrible, uncompromising instrument, to carry England over such a crisis as was before her. Not overscrupulous about means, no troublesome theories about Church or State—no reverence for anything but God and "the Gospel. "

When Parliament halted and hesitated at the last about the trial of the King, it was the iron hand of Cromwell which strangled opposition, by placing a body of troops at the door, and excluding 140 doubtful members. A Parliament, with the House of Lords effaced, and with 140 obstructing members excluded, leaving only a small body of men of the same mind, sustained by the moral sentiment of a Cromwellian Army, —can scarcely be called a Representative body; nor can it be considered competent to create a Court for the trial of a King! It was only justifiable as a last and desperate measure of self-defence.

[Sidenote: Death of Charles I., 1649]

Charles wins back some of our sympathy and esteem by dying like a brave man and a gentleman. He conducted himself with marvellous dignity and self-possession throughout the trial, and at the end of seven days, laid his head upon the block in front of his royal palace of Whitehall.

That small body of men, calling itself the "House of Commons, " declared England a "Commonwealth, " which was to be governed without any King or House of Lords. Cromwell was "Lord Protector of England, Scotland and Ireland. " He scorned to be called King, but no King was ever more absolute in authority. It was a righteous tyranny, replacing a vicious one.

There was no longer an eager hand dipping into the pockets of the people, compelling the poor to share his scanty earnings with the King. There was safety, and there was prosperity. But there was rage and detestation, as Cromwell's soldiers with gibes and jeers, hewed and hacked at venerable altars and pictures, and insulted the religious sentiment of one-half the people. Empty niches, mutilated carvings, and fragments of stained glass, from

> "Windows richly dight,
> Casting a dim religious light, "

show us to-day the track of those profane fanatics.

[Sidenote: Long Parliament Dispersed.]

When the remnant of the House of Commons calling itself a Parliament was not alert enough in its obedience, Cromwell marched into the Hall with a company of musketeers, and calling them names neither choice nor flattering, ordered them to "get out, " then locked the door, and put the key into his pocket. Such was the "dissolution" of a Parliament which had been strong enough to overthrow a Government, and to send a King to the scaffold! This might be fittingly described as a *personal* Government!

He was loved by none but the Army. There was no strong current of popular sentiment to uphold him as he carried out his arbitrary purposes; no engines of cruelty to fortify his authority; no "Star Chamber" to enforce his order. Men were not being nailed by the ears to the pillory, nor mutilated and branded, for resisting his will. But the spectacle was for that reason all the more astonishing: a great nation, full of rage, hate and bitterness, but silent and submissive under the spell of one dominating personality.

He had no experience in diplomatic usages, no skilled ministers to counsel and warn, but by his foreign policy he made himself the terror of Europe; Spain, France, and the United Provinces courting his friendship, while Protestantism had protection at home and abroad.

That the man who did this had a commanding genius, all must be agreed. But whether he was the incarnation of evil, or of righteousness, must ever remain in dispute. We shall never know whether or not his death, in 1658, cut short a career which might have passed from a justifiable to an unjustifiable tyranny.

[Sidenote: Charles II., 1660.]

A fabric held up by one sustaining hand, must fall when that hand is withdrawn. Cromwell left none who could support his burden. Charles II., who had been more than once foiled in trying to get in by the back door of his father's kingdom, was now invited to enter by the front, and amid shouts of joy was placed on the throne.

CHAPTER X.

Time brings its revenges. The instinct for beauty, and for joy and gladness, had been for twenty-one years repressed by harshly administered Puritanism. There was a thrill of delight in greeting a gracious, smiling king, who would lift the spell of gloom from the nation. Charles did this, more fully than was expected. Never was the law of reaction more fully demonstrated! The Court was profligate, and the age licentious. The reign of Charles was an orgy. When he needed more money for his pleasures, he bargained with Louis XIV. to join him in a war upon Protestantism in Holland, for the consideration of 200,000 pounds!

We wonder how he dared thus to goad and prod the British Lion, which had devoured his Father. But that animal had grown patient since the Protectorate. England treated Charles like a spoiled child whose follies entertained her, and whose misdemeanors she had not the heart to punish.

[Sidenote: Act of Habeas Corpus, 1679.]

The "Roundheads, " who had trampled upon the "Cavaliers, " were now trampled upon in return. But even at such a time as this the liberties of the people were expanding. The Act of "Habeas Corpus" forever prevented imprisonment, without showing in Court just cause for the detention of the prisoner.

[Sidenote: Death of Charles II., 1685.] The House of Stuart, those children of the Guises, was always Catholic at heart, and Charles was at no pains to conceal his preferences. A wave of Catholicism alarmed the people, who tried to divert the succession from James, the brother of the King, who was extreme and fanatical in his devotion to the Church of Rome. But in 1685, the Masks and routs and revels were interrupted. The pleasure-loving Charles, who "had never said a foolish thing, and never done a wise one, " lay dead in his palace at Whitehall, and James II. was King of England.

[Sidenote: Milton and Bunyan.]

Three names have illumined this reign, in other respects so inglorious. In 1666 Newton discovered the law of gravitation and created a new theory of the Universe. In 1667 Milton published

The Evolution of an Empire

"Paradise Lost, " and in 1672 Bunyan gave to the world his allegory, "Pilgrim's Progress. " There was no inspiration to genius in the cause of King and Cavaliers. But the stern problems of Puritanism touched two souls with the divine afflatus. The sacred Epic of Milton, sublime in treatment as in conception, must ever stand unique and solitary in literature; while "Pilgrim's Progress, " in plain homely dish served the same heavenly food. The theme of both was the problem of sin and redemption with which the Puritan soul was gloomily struggling.

The reign of James II. was the last effort of royal despotism to recover its own. He tried to recall the right of Habeas Corpus; —to efface Parliament—and to overawe the Clergy, while insidiously striving to establish Papacy as the religion of the Kingdom. Chief Justice Jeffries, that most brutal of men, was his efficient aid, and boasted that he had in the service of James hanged more traitors than all his predecessors since the Conquest!

The names Whig and Tory had come into existence in this struggle. Whig, standing for the opponents to Catholic domination, and Tory for the upholders of the King. But so flagrantly was the Catholic policy of James conducted, that his upholders were few. In three years from his accession, Whig and Tory alike were so alarmed, that they secretly sent an invitation to the King's son-in-law, William, Prince of Orange, to come and accept the Crown.

[Sidenote: James II. Deposed.]

William responded at once, and when he landed with 14,000 men, James, paralyzed, powerless, unable to raise a force to meet him, abandoned his throne without a struggle and took refuge in France.

[Sidenote: William and Mary, 1689-1702.]

The throne was formally declared vacant and William and Mary his wife were invited to rule jointly the Kingdom of England, Ireland and Scotland (1689).

The House of Stuart, which seems to have brought not one single virtue to the throne, was always secretly conspiring with Catholicism in Europe. Louis XIV., as the head of Catholic Europe at this time, was the natural protector of the dethroned King. His aim had long been, to bring England into the Catholic European alliance, and, of

The Evolution of an Empire

course, if possible, to make it a dependency of France. A conspiracy with Louis to accomplish this end occupied England's exiled King during the rest of his life.

[Sidenote: Battle of Boyne, 1690.]

But European Protestantism had for its leader the man who now sat upon the throne of England. In fact he had probably accepted that throne in order to further his larger plans for defeating the expanding power of Louis XIV. in Europe. Broad and comprehensive in his statesmanship, noble and just in character, an able military leader, England was safe in his strong hand. Conspiracies were put down, one French army after another, with the despicable James at its head, was driven back; the purpose at one time being to establish James at the head of an independent Kingdom in Catholic Ireland. But that would-be King of Ireland was humiliated and sent back to France by the battle of Boyne Battle of Boyne (1690).

[Sidenote: Bill of Rights]

As important as was all this, things of even greater moment were going on in the life of England at this time. As a wise householder employs the hours of sunshine to repair the leaks revealed by the storm, just so Parliament now set about strengthening and riveting the weak spots revealed by the storms which had swept over England.

What the *"Magna Charta"* and *"Petition of Right"* had asserted in a general way, was now by the *"Bill of Rights, "* established by specific enactments, which one after another declared what the King should and what he should not do. One of these Acts touched the very central nerve of English freedom.

If *religion* and *money* are the two important factors in the life of a nation, it is *money* upon which its life from day to day depends! A Government can exist without money about as long as a man without air! So the act which gave to the House of Commons exclusive power to grant supplies, and also to determine to what use they shall be applied, transferred the real authority to the people, whose will the Commons express.

The struggle between the Crown and Parliament ends with this, and the theory of Pym is vindicated. The Sovereign and the House of

Lords from that time could no more take money from the Treasury of England, than from that of France. Henceforth there can be no differences between King and people. *They must be friends.* A Ministry which forfeits the friendship of the Commons, cannot stand an hour, and supplies will stop until they are again in accord. In other words, the Government of England had become a Government *of the people*.

William regarded these enactments as evidence of a lack of confidence in him. Conscious of his own magnanimous aims, of his power and his purpose to serve England as she had not been served before, he felt hurt and wounded at fetters which had not been placed upon such Kings as Charles I. and his sons. We wonder that a man so exalted and so superior, did not see that it was for future England that these laws were framed, for a time when perhaps a Prince not generous, and noble, and pure should be upon the throne.

William was silent, grave, cold, reserved almost to sternness. He had none of the qualities which awaken personal enthusiasm. He was one of those great leaders who are worshipped from afar. Besides, it is not an easy task to rule another's household. Benefits however great, reforms however wise, are sure to be considered an impertinence by some. Then— there might be another "Restoration, " and wary ambitious nobles were cautiously making a record which would not unfit them for its benefits when it came. He lived in an atmosphere of conspiracy, suspicion, and loyalty grudgingly bestowed. But these were only the surface currents. Anglo-Saxon England recognized in this foreign King, a man with the same race instincts, the same ideals of integrity, honor, justice and personal liberty, as her own; qualities possessed by few of her native sovereigns since the good King Alfred.

The expensive wars carried on against James and his confederate, Louis XIV., compelled loans which were the beginning of the National Debt. That and the establishing of the Bank of England, form part of the history of this reign.

In 1702 William died, and Mary having also died a few years earlier, the succession passed to her sister Anne, who was to be the last Sovereign of the House of Stuart.

CHAPTER XI.

[Sidenote: Anne, Queen of England.]

William's policy had not been bounded by his Island Kingdom. It included the cause of Protestant Europe. An apparently invincible King sat on the throne of France, gradually drawing all adjacent Kingdoms into his dominion. When in defiance of past pledges he placed his grandson upon the vacant throne of Spain, and declared that the Pyrenees should exist no more, even Catholic Austria revolted, and beginning to fear Louis more than Protestantism, new combinations were formed, England still holding aloof, and striving to keep out of the Alliance. But that all-absorbing King had long ago fixed his eye upon England as his future prey, and when he refused to recognize Anne as lawful Queen and declared his intention of placing the "Pretender" (illegitimate son of James) upon the throne, there could be no more hesitation. This Jupiter who had removed the Pyrenees, might wipe out the English Channel too! Hitherto the name Whig had stood for the adherents to the war policy, and Tory for its opponents. Now, all was changed. Even the stupid Anne and her Tory friends saw that William's policy must be her policy if she would keep her Kingdom.

[Sidenote: Marlborough.]

Fortunate was it for England, and for Europe at this time that a "Marlborough" had climbed to distinction by a slender, and not too reputable ladder. This man, John Churchill, who a few years ago had been unknown, without training, almost without education, was by pure genius fitted to become, upon the death of William, the guiding spirit of the Grand Alliance.

He had none of the qualities possessed by William, and all the qualities that leader had not. He had no moral grandeur, no stern adherence to principles. Whig and Tory were alike to him, and he followed whichever seemed to lead to success, and to the richest rewards. He was perfectly sordid in his aims, invincible in his good nature, with a careless, easy *bonhomie* which captured the hearts of Europeans, who called him "the handsome Englishman. " As adroit in managing men as armies, as wise in planning political moves as campaigns, using tact and diplomacy as effectually as artillery, he assumed the whole direction of the European war; managed every negotiation, planned every battle, and achieved its great and overwhelming success.

[Sidenote: "Battle of Blenheim, 1704."]

"Blenheim" turned the tide of French victory, and broke the spell of Louis' invincibility. The loss at that battle was something more than men and fortresses. It was *prestige,* and that self-confidence which had made the great King believe that nothing could resist his purposes. It was a new sensation for him to bend his neck, and to say that he acknowledged Anne Queen of England.

Marlborough received as his reward the splendid estate upon which was built the palace of "Blenheim. " Then, when in the sunshine of peace England needed him no more, Anne quarrelled with his wife, her adored friend, and cast him aside as a rusty sword no longer of use. But for years Europe heard the song "Malbrook s'en va-t-en guerre, " and his awe-inspiring name was used to frighten children in France and in England.

His passionate love for his wife, Sarah Churchill, ran like a golden thread of romance through Marlborough's stormy career. On the eve of battle, and in the first flush of victory, he must first and last write her; and he would more willingly meet 20,000 Frenchmen than his wife's displeasure! Indeed Sarah seems to have waged her own battles very successfully with her tongue, and also to have had her own diplomatic triumphs. Through Anne's infatuation for her, she was virtually ruler while the friendship lasted. But to acquire ascendancy over Anne was not much of an achievement.

It is said that there was but one duller person than the Queen in her Kingdom, and that was the royal Consort, George, Prince of Denmark. Happy was it for England that of the seventeen children born into this royal household, not one survived. The succession, in the absence of Anne's heirs, was pledged to George, Elector of Hanover, a remote descendant of James I.

It was during Anne's reign that English literature assumed a new character. The stately and classic form being set aside for a style more familiar, and which concerned itself with the affairs of everyday life. Letters showed with a mild splendor, while Steele, Sterne, Swift, Defoe and Fielding were writing, and Addison's "Spectator" was on every breakfast-table.

The Evolution of an Empire

[Sidenote: Anne died, 1714.]

In the year 1714 Anne died, and George I, of the House of Hanover, was King of England, —an England which, thanks to the great soldier and Duke, would never more be molested by the intriguing designs of a French King, and which held in her hand Gibraltar, the key to the Mediterranean.

[Sidenote: House of Hanover, 1714. George I.]

King George I. was a German grandson of Elizabeth, sister of Charles I. Deeply attached to his own Hanover, this stupid old man came slowly and reluctantly to assume his new honors. He could not speak English; and as he smoked his long pipe, his homesick soul was soothed by the ladies of his Court, who cut caricature figures out of paper for his amusement, while Robert Walpole relieved him of affairs of State. As ignorant of the politics of England as of its language, Walpole selected the King's Ministers and determined the policy of his Government; establishing a precedent which has always been followed. Since that time it has been the duty of the Prime Minister to form the Ministry; and no sovereign since Anne has ever appeared at a Cabinet Council, nor has refused assent to a single Act of Parliament.

[Sidenote: Whig rule.]

Such a King was merely a symbol of Protestantism and of Constitutional Government. But this stream of royal dulness which set in from Hanover in 1714, came as a great blessing at the time. It enabled England to be ruled for thirty years by the party which had since the usurpation of James I. stood for the rights of the people. Walpole created a Whig Government. The Whigs had never wavered from certain principles upon which they had risen to power. There must be no tampering with justice, nor with the freedom of the press, nor any attempt to rule independently of Parliament. Thirty years of rule under these principles converted them into an integral part of the national life. The habit of loyalty to them was so established by this long Government of the Whig party, that Englishmen forgot such things could be, that it was possible to infringe upon the sacred liberties of the people.

However much "Whig" and "Tory" have seemed to change since we first hear of them in the time of James I., they have in fact remained

The Evolution of an Empire

essentially the same; the Whigs always tending to limit the power of the crown, and the Tories to limit that of the people. At the time of Walpole the Tories had been the supporters of the Pretender and of the High Church party, the Whigs of the policy of William and Protestantism. Their predecessors were the "Cavaliers" and "Roundheads, " and their successors to-day are found in the "Liberals" and "Conservatives. "

[Sidenote: South-Sea Bubble, 1720.]

There was at last peace abroad and prosperity at home. The latter was interrupted for a time in 1720 by the speculative madness created by the "South-Sea Bubble. " Men were almost crazed by the rise in the value of shares from 100 pounds to 1,000 pounds; and then plunged into despair and ruin when they suddenly dropped to nothing. The suffering caused by this wreck of fortunes was great. But industries revived, and prosperity and wealth returned with little to disturb them again until the death of George I. in 1727; when another George came over from Hanover to occupy the English throne.

[Sidenote: Death of George, 1727.]

George II. had one advantage over his father. He did speak the English language. Nor was he content to smoke his pipe and entrust his Kingdom to his Ministers, which was a doubtful advantage for the nation. But his clever wife, Queen Caroline, believed thoroughly in Walpole, and when she was controlled by the Minister, and then in turn herself controlled the policy of the King, that simple gentleman supposed that he, —George II., —was ruling his own Kingdom. His small, narrow mind was incapable of statesmanship; but he was a good soldier. Methodical, stubborn and passionate, he was a King who needed to be carefully watched, and adroitly managed, to keep him from doing harm.

[Sidenote: The "Young Pretender. " Culloden Moor, 1746.]

There was a young "Pretender" in these days (Charles Edward Stuart), who was conspiring with Louis XV., as his father had done with Louis XIV., to get to the English throne. We see him flitting about Europe from time to time, landing here and there on the British Coast—until when finally defeated at "Culloden Moor, " 1746, this wraith of the House of Stuart disappears—dying obscurely

The Evolution of an Empire

in Rome; and "Wha'll be King but Charlie, " and "Over the Water to Charlie, " linger only as the echo of a lost cause.

[Sidenote: "Seven Years' War. "]

There was a time of despondency when England seemed to be annexed to Hanover, following her fortunes, and sharing her misfortunes in the "seven years' war" over the Austrian succession, as if the Great Kingdom were a mere dependency to the little Electorate; and all to please the stubborn King. Desiring peace above all things England was no sooner freed from one entanglement, than she was plunged into another.

In India, the English "Merchant Company, " chartered by Elizabeth in 1600, had expanded to a power. One of the native Princes, jealous of these foreign intruders in Bengal, and roused, it was said, by the French to expel them, committed that deed at which the world has shuddered ever since. One hundred and fifty settlers and traders, were thrust into an air-tight dungeon—an Indian midsummer. Maddened with heat and with thirst, most of them died before morning, trampling upon each other in frantic efforts to get air and water. This is the story of the "Black Hole of Calcutta; " which led to the victories of Clive, and the establishment of English Empire in India, 1757.

[Sidenote: British Dominion in India, 1757. Battle of Quebec, 1760.]

Two years later a quarrel over the boundaries of their American colonies brought the French and English into direct conflict. Gen. Wolfe, the English Commander, was killed at the moment of victory in scaling the walls of Quebec. Montcalm, the French commander, being saved the humiliation of seeing the loss of Canada (1760), by sharing the same fate.

The dream of French Empire in America was at an end; and with the cession of Florida by Spain, England was mistress of the eastern half of the Continent from Nova Scotia to the Gulf of Mexico, and from the Atlantic to the Mississippi. So since the days of Elizabeth, and from seed dropped by her hand, an Eastern and a Western Empire had been added to that island Kingdom, whose highest dream had been to get back some of her lost provinces in France. Instead of that it was to be her destiny to girdle the Earth, so that the Sun in its entire course should never cease to shine upon British Dominions.

The Evolution of an Empire

[Sidenote: John Wesley.]

Side by side with the aspiration which uplifts a nation, there is always a tendency toward degradation, which can only be arrested by the infusion of a higher spiritual life. Strong alcoholic liquors had taken the place of beer in England (to avoid the excessive tax imposed upon it) and the grossest intemperance prevailed in the early part of this reign. John Wesley introduced a regenerative force when he went about among the people preaching "Methodism, " a pure and simple religion. Not since Augustine had the hearts of men been so touched, and a new life and new spirit came into being, better than all the prosperity and territorial expansion of the time.

Walpole had passed from view long before the stirring changes we have alluded to. A new hand was guiding the affairs of State; the hand of William Pitt.

CHAPTER XII.

At the close of the Seven Years' War, England had driven the French out of Canada, —her ships which had traversed the Pacific from one end to the other, (Capt. Cook) had wherever they touched, claimed islands for the Crown; she had projected into the heart of India English institutions and civilization.

Mistress of North America, and of the Pacific Isles, and future mistress of India, she had left in comparative insignificance those European States whose power was bounded by a single Continent. And all this, —in the reign of the puniest King who had ever sat upon her throne! As if to show that England was great not through— but in spite of, her Kings.

[Sidenote: George III. 1760-1820.]

When in 1760, George III. came to the throne, thirteen prosperous American Colonies were a source of handsome revenue to the mother country, by whom they were regarded as receptacles for surplus population, and a good field for unsuccessful men and adventurers. These children were frequently reminded that they owed England a great debt of gratitude. They had cost her expensive Indian and French wars for which she should expect them to reimburse her as their prosperity grew. They were to make nothing themselves, not so much as a horseshoe; but to send their raw material to English mills and factories, and when it was returned to them in wares and manufactured articles, they were to pay such taxes as were imposed, with grateful hearts to the kind Government which was so good as to rule them.

[Sidenote: Stamp Act, 1765.]

If the Colonies had still needed the protection of England from the French, they might never have questioned the propriety of their treatment. They were at heart intensely loyal, and the thought of severance from the Mother Country probably did not exist in a single breast. But they had since the fall of Quebec a feeling of security which was a good background for independence, if their manhood required its assertion. They were Anglo-Saxons, and perfectly understood the long struggle for civil rights which lay behind them. So when in 1765 they were told that they must bear their share of the burden of National Debt which had been increased by wars in their behalf, and to that end a "Stamp Act" had been passed, they very carefully looked into the demand. This Act required that every legal document drawn in the Colonies, will, deed, note, draft, receipt, etc., be written upon paper bearing an expensive Government stamp.

The thirteen Colonies, utterly at variance upon most subjects, were upon this agreed: *They would not submit to the tax.* They had read the Magna Charta, they knew that the Stamp Act violated its most vital principle. This tax had been framed to extort money from men who had no representation in Parliament, hence without their consent.

Pitt vehemently declared that the Act was a tyranny, Burke and Fox protested against it, the brain and the heart of England compelled the repeal of the Act; Pitt declaring that the spirit shown in America was the same that in England had withstood the Stuarts, and refused "Ship Money. " There was rejoicing and ringing of bells over the repeal, but before the echoes had died away another plan was forming in the narrow recesses of the King's brain.

George III. had read English History. He remembered that if Parliaments grow obstructive, the way is not to fight them but to pack them with the right kind of material. Tampering with the boroughs, had so filled the House of Commons with Tories that it had almost ceased to be a representative body, and if Pitt would not bow to his wishes, he would find a Minister who would. Another tax was devised.

[Sidenote: Tax on Tea.]

Threepence a pound upon tea, shipped direct to America from India, would save the impost to England, bring tea at a cheaper rate to the Colonies (even with the added tax), and at the same time yield a handsome revenue to the Government.

The Colonists were not at all moved by the idea of getting cheaper tea. They had taken their stand in this matter of taxation without representation; they would never move from it one inch. When the cargo of tea arrived in Boston harbor, it was thrown overboard by men disguised as Indians.

The Evolution of an Empire

George III. in a rage closed the port of Boston, cancelled the Charter of Massachusetts, withdrew the right of electing its own council and judges, investing the *Governor* with these rights, to whom he also gave the power to send rebellious and seditious prisoners to England for trial. Then to make all this sure of fulfilment, he sent troops to enforce the order, in command of General Gage, whom he also appointed *Governor* of Massachusetts.

Fox said, "How intolerable that it should be in the power of one blockhead to do so much mischief! " The obstinacy of George III. cost England her dearest and fairest possession. It is almost impossible to picture what would be her power to-day if she had continued to be mistress of North America!

All unconscious of his stupendous folly, the King was delighted at his own firmness. He rubbed his hands in high glee as he said, — "The die is cast, the Colonies must submit or triumph, " meaning of course that "triumph" was a thing impossible. Pitt (now Earl Chatham), Burke, Fox, even the Tory House of Lords, petitioned and implored in vain. The confident, stubborn King stood alone, and upon him lies the whole responsibility—Lord North simply acting as his compliant tool.

The colonies united as one, all local differences forgotten. As they fought at Lexington and at Bunker Hill, the idea of something more than *resistance* was born—the idea of *independence*.

A letter from the Government addressed to the Commander-in-Chief as "George Washington, Esq., " was sent back unopened. Battles were lost and won, the courage and resources of the Americans holding out for years as if by miracle, until when reinforced by France the end drew near; and was reached with the defeat of Lord Cornwallis at Yorktown.

[Sidenote: Independence Acknowledged, 1782.]

It was a dreary morning in 1782 when a humiliated King stood before the House of Lords and acknowledged the independence of the United States of America!

Thus ended a contest which the Earl of Chatham had said "was conceived in injustice, and nurtured in folly. "

The Evolution of an Empire

It was during the American war that the Press rose to be a great counterbalancing power. Popular sentiment no longer finding an outlet in the House of Commons, sought another mode of expression. Public opinion gathered in by the newspapers became a force before which Government dared not stand. The "Chronicle, " "Post, " "Herald" and "Times" came into existence, philosophers like Coleridge, and statesmen like Canning using their columns and compelling reforms.

[Sidenote: Impeachment of Warren Hastings, 1788.]

The impeachment of Warren Hastings, conducted by Burke, Sheridan, and Fox, led to such an exposure of the cruelty and corruption of the East India Company, that the gigantic monopoly was broken up. A "Board of Control" was created for the administration of Indian affairs, thus absorbing it into the general system of English Government (1784).

James Watt had introduced (in 1769) steam into the life of England, with consequences dire at first, and fraught with such tremendous results later, changing all the industrial conditions of England and of the world.

In 1789 England witnessed that terrific outburst of human passions in France, which culminated in the death of a King and a Queen. An appalling sight which made Republicanism seem odious, even to so exalted and just a soul as Burke, who denounced it with words of thrilling eloquence. Then came Napoleon Bonaparte, and his swift ascent to imperial power, followed by his audacious conquest almost of Europe, until Arthur Wellesley, the Duke of Wellington, led the allied army at Waterloo, and Napoleon's sun went down.

In 1812 the United States for a second time declared war against England. That country had claimed the right to search for British-born seamen upon American ships, in order to impress them into her own service and recruit her Navy. The "right of search" was denied, and the British forces landed in Maryland, burned the Capitol and Congressional Library at Washington, but met their "Waterloo" at New Orleans, where, under General Andrew Jackson, they were defeated, and the "right of search" is heard of no more.

Long before this time George III. had been a prey to blindness, deafness, and insanity, and in 1820 his death came as a welcome event. Had he not been blind, deaf, and insane, in 1775, England might not have lost her fairest possession.

The weight of the enormous debt incurred by the long wars fell most heavily upon the poor. One-half of their earnings went to the Crown. The poor man lived under a taxed roof, wore taxed clothing, ate taxed food from taxed dishes, and looked at the light of day through taxed window-glass. Nothing was free but the ocean.

But there must not be cheap bread, for that meant reduced rents. The farmer was "protected" by having the price of corn kept artificially above a certain point, and further "protected" by a prohibitory tax upon foreign corn, all in order that the landlord might collect undiminished rentals from his farm lands. But, alas! there was no "protection" from starvation. Is it strange that gaunt famine was a frequent visitor in the land? —But men must starve in silence. —To beg was crime.

> "Alas, that bread should be so dear,
> And flesh and blood so cheap! "

Children six years old worked fourteen and fifteen hours daily in mines and factories, beaten by overseers to keep them awake over their tasks; while others five and six years old, driven by blows, crawled with their brooms into narrow soot-clogged chimneys, and sometimes getting wedged in narrow flues, were mercifully suffocated and translated to a kinder world.

A ruinous craving was created for stimulants, which took the place of insufficient food, and in these stunted, pallid, emaciated beings a foundation was laid for an enfeebled and debased population, which would sorely tax the wisdom of statesmanship in the future.

If such was the condition of the honest working poor, what was that of the criminal? It is difficult now to comprehend the ferocity of laws which made *235 offenses—punishable with death*, —most of which we should now call misdemeanors. But perhaps death was better than the prisons, which were the abode of vermin, disease and filth unspeakable. Jailers asked for no pay, but depended upon the money they could wring from the wretched beings in their charge for food and small alleviations to their misery. In 1773 John Howard commenced his work in the prisons, and the idea was first conceived that the object of punishment should be not to degrade sin-sick humanity, but to reform it.

Far above this deep dark undercurrent, there was a bright, shining surface. Johnson had made his ponderous contribution to letters. Francis Barney had surprised the world with "Evelina; " Horace Walpole, (son of Sir Robert) was dropping witty epigrams from his pen; Sheridan, Goldsmith, Cowper, Burns, Southey, Coleridge, Wordsworth, in tones both grave and gay, were making sweet music; while Scott, Byron, Shelley added strains rich and melodious.

[Sidenote: First English Railway, 1830.]

As all this was passing, George Stephenson was pondering over a daring project. Fulton had completed his invention in 1807, and in 1819 the first steamship had crossed the Atlantic. If engines could be made to plough through the water, why might they not also be made to walk the earth? It was thought an audacious experiment when he put this iron fire-devouring monster on wheels, to draw loaded cars. Not until 1830 was his plan realized, when his new locomotive—"The Rocket"—drew the first railway train from Liverpool to Manchester, the Duke of Wellington venturing his life on the trial trip.

In the year 1782 Ireland was permitted to have its own Parliament; but owing to a treasonable correspondence with France, a few years later, she was deprived of this legislative independence, and in 1801, after a prolonged struggle, was reunited to Great Britain, and thenceforth sent her representatives to the British Parliament.

[Sidenote: Oppression of Roman Catholics. Daniel O'Connell.]

The laws against Roman Catholics which had been enacted as measures of self-defence from the Stuarts, now that there was no longer a necessity for them had become an oppression, which bore with special weight upon Catholic Ireland. By the oath of "Supremacy, " and by the declarations against transubstantiation, intercession of Saints, etc., etc., the Catholics were shut out from all share in a Government which they were taxed to support. Such an obvious injustice should not have needed a powerful pleader; but it found one in Daniel O'Connell, who by constant agitation and fiery eloquence created such a public sentiment, that the Ministry, headed by the Duke of Wellington, aided by Sir Robert Peel in the House,

The Evolution of an Empire

carried through a measure in 1828 which opened Parliament to Catholics, and also gave them free access to all places of trust, Civil or Military, —excepting that of Regent, —Lord Chancellor—and Lord Lieutenant of Ireland.

[Sidenote: George IV., 1820-1830.]

There is nothing to record of George IV. except the irregularities of his private life, over which we need not linger. He was a dissolute spendthrift. His illegal marriage with Mrs. Fitzherbert, and his legal marriage with Caroline of Brunswick from whom he quickly freed himself, are the chief events in his history.

His charming young daughter, the Princess Charlotte, had died in 1817, soon after her marriage with Prince Leopold of Saxe-Coburg. She had been adored as the future Queen, but upon the death of George IV. in 1830, the Crown passed to his sailor brother William.

[Sidenote: William IV., 1830-1837.]

William IV. was sixty-five when he came to the throne. He was not a courtier in his manners, nor much of a fine gentleman in his tastes. But his plain, rough sincerity was not unacceptable, and his immediate espousal of the Reform Act, then pending, won him popularity at once.

The efficiency and integrity of the House of Commons had long been impaired by an effete system of representation, which had been unchanged for 500 years. Boroughs were represented which had long disappeared from the face of the earth. One had for years been covered by the sea! Another existed as a fragment of a wall in a gentleman's park, while towns like Manchester, Leeds, Birmingham, and nineteen other large and prosperous places, had no representation whatever. These "rotten boroughs" as they were called, were usually in the hands of wealthy landowners; one great Peer literally carrying eleven boroughs in his pocket, so that eleven members went to the House of Commons at his dictation. —It would seem that a reform so obviously needed should have been easy to accomplish. But the House of Lords clung to the old system as if the life of the Kingdom depended upon it. And when the measure was finally carried the good old Duke of Wellington said sadly, "We must hope for the best; but the most sanguine cannot believe we shall ever again be as prosperous."

By this Act 56 boroughs were disfranchised, and 43 new ones, with 30 county constituencies, were created.

[Sidenote: "Reform Bill, 1832"]

It was in the contest over this Reform Bill that the Tories took the name of "Conservatives" and their opponents "Liberals." Its passage marks a most important transition in England. The workingman was by it enfranchised, and the House of Commons, which had hitherto represented *property*, thenceforth represented *manhood*.

Nor were political reforms the only ones. Human pity awoke from its lethargy. The penalties for wrongdoing became less brutal, the prisons less terrible. No longer did gaping crowds watch shivering wretches brought out of the jails every Monday morning, in batches of twenty and thirty, to be hung for pilfering or something even less. Little children were lifted out of the mines and factories and chimneys and placed in schools, which also began to be created for the poor. Numberless ways were devised for making life less miserable for the unfortunate, and for improving the social conditions of toiling men and women.

[Sidenote: Slaves Emancipated, 1833.]

While white slavery in the collieries and factories was thus mitigated, Wilberforce removed the stain of negro slavery from England in securing the passage of a Bill which, while compensating the owners (who received 20,000,000 pounds), set 800,000 human beings free (1833).

The Evolution of an Empire

CHAPTER XIII.

[Sidenote: Accession of Victoria, 1837.]

William IV. died at Windsor Castle, and at 5 o'clock on the morning of June 2oth, 1837 (just 58 years from the day this is written), a young girl of eighteen was awakened to be told she was Queen of Great Britain and Ireland. Victoria was the only child of Edward, Duke of Kent, brother of William IV. Her marriage in 1840 with her cousin, Prince Albert of Saxe-Coburg, was one of deep affection, and secured for her a wise and prudent counsellor.

[Sidenote: Famine in Ireland, 1846.]

On account of the high price of corn, Ireland had for years subsisted entirely upon potatoes. The failure of this crop for several successive seasons, in 1846 produced a famine of such appalling dimensions that the old and the new world came to the rescue of the starving people. Parliament voted 10,000,000 pounds for food. But before relief could reach them, two millions, one-fourth of the population of Ireland, had perished. The anti-corn measures, championed by Richard Cobden and John Bright, which had been bitterly opposed by the Tories under the leadership of Disraeli, were thus reinforced by unexpected argument; foreign breadstuffs were permitted free access and free trade was accepted as the policy of England.

Nicholas, the Czar of Russia, was, after the fashion of his predecessors (and his successors), always waiting for the right moment to sweep down upon Constantinople. England had become only a land of shopkeepers, France was absorbed with her new Empire, and with trying on her fresh imperial trappings. The time seemed favorable for a move. The pious soul of Nicholas was suddenly stirred by certain restrictions laid by the Sultan upon the Christians in Palestine. He demanded that he be made the Protector of Christianity in the Turkish Empire, by an arrangement which would in fact transfer the Sovereignty from Constantinople to St. Petersburg.

That mass of Oriental corruption known as the Ottoman Empire, held together by no vital forces, was ready to fall into ruin at one vigorous touch. It was an anachronism in modern Europe, where its cruelty was only limited by its weakness. That such an odious,

The Evolution of an Empire

treacherous despotism should so strongly appeal to the sympathies of England that she was willing to enter upon a life-and-death struggle for its maintenance, let those believe who can. —Her rushing to the defence of Turkey, was about as sincere as Russia's interest in the Christians in Palestine.

The simple truth beneath all these diplomatic subterfuges was of course that Russia wanted Constantinople, and England would at any cost prevent her getting it. The keys to the East must, in any event, not belong to Russia, her only rival in Asia.

France had no Eastern Empire to protect, so her participation in the struggle is at first not so easy to comprehend, until we reflect that she had an ambitious and *parvenu* Emperor. To have Europe see him in confidential alliance with England, was alone worth a war; while a vigorous foreign policy would help to divert attention from the recent treacheries by which he had reached a throne.

[Sidenote: War with Russia, 1854.]

Such were some of the hidden springs of action which in 1854 brought about the Crimean War, —one of the most deadly and destructive of modern times. Two great Christian kingdoms had rushed to the defence of the worst Government ever known, and the best blood in England was being poured into Turkish soil.

The Russians soon found that the English were no less skilled as fighters, than as shopkeepers. They were victorious from the very first, even when the numbers were ill-matched. But one immortal deed of valor must have made her tremble before the spirit it revealed.

Six hundred cavalrymen, in obedience to an order which all knew was a blunder, dashed into a valley lined with cannon, and charged an army of 30,000 men!

> "Was there a man dismayed?
> Not though the soldiers knew
> Some one had blundered.
> Theirs not to reason why,
> Theirs but to do, —and die,
> As into the Valley of Death
> Rode the six hundred."

The Evolution of an Empire

The horrible blunder at Balaklava was not the only one. One incapable general was followed by another, and routine and red-tape were more deadly than Russian shot and shell.

Food and supplies beyond their utmost power of consumption, were hurried to the army by grateful England. Thousands of tons of wood for huts, shiploads of clothing and profuse provision for health and comfort, reached Balaklava.

While the tall masts of the ships bearing these treasures were visible from the heights of Sebastopol, men there were perishing for lack of food, fuel and clothing. In rags, almost barefoot, half-fed, often without fuel even to cook their food, in that terrible winter on the heights, whole regiments of heroes became extinct, because there was not sufficient administrative ability to convey the supplies to a perishing army!

So wretched was the hospital service, that to be sent there meant death. Gangrene carried off four out of five. Men were dying at a rate which would have extinguished the entire army in a year and a half. It was Florence Nightingale who redeemed this national disgrace, and brought order, care and healing into the camps.

When England recalls with pride the valor and the victories in the Crimea, let her remember it was the *manhood in the ranks* which achieved it. When all was over, war had slain its thousands, —but official incapacity its tens of thousands!

It was a costly victory: Russia was humiliated, was even shut out from the waters of her own Black Sea, where she had hitherto been supreme. To two million Turks was preserved the privilege of oppressing eight million Christians; and for this, —twenty thousand British youth had perished. But—the way to India was unobstructed!

England's career of conquest in India was not altogether of her own seeking. As a neighboring province committed outrages upon its British neighbors, it became necessary in self-defence to punish it; and such punishment, invariably led to its subjugation. In this way one province after another was subdued, until finally in the absorption of the Kingdom of Oude (1856) the natural boundary of the Himalaya Mountains had been reached, and the conquest was complete. The little trading company of British merchants had become an Empire, vast and rich beyond the wildest dreams of romance.

The British rule was upon the whole beneficent. The condition of the people was improved, and there was little dissatisfaction except among the deposed native princes, who were naturally filled with hate and bitterness. The large army required to hold such an amount of territory, was to a great extent recruited from the native population, the Sepoys, as they were called, making good soldiers.

[Sidenote: Sepoy Rebellion, 1857-1858.]

In 1857 the King of the Oude and some of the native princes cunningly devised a plan of undermining the British by means of their Sepoys, and circumstances afforded a singular opportunity for carrying out their design.

A new rifle had been adopted, which required a greased cartridge, for which animal grease was used. The Sepoys were told this was a deep-laid plot to overthrow their native religions. The Mussulman was to be eternally lost by defiling his lips with the fat of swine, and the Hindu, by the indignity offered to the venerated Cow. These English had tried to ruin them not alone in this world, but in the next.

[Sidenote: Massacre at Cawnpore.]

Thrilled with horror, terror-stricken, the dusky soldiers were converted into demons. Mutinies arose simultaneously at twenty-two stations; not only officers, but Europeans, were slaughtered without mercy. At Cawnpore was the crowning horror. After a siege of many days the garrison capitulated to Nana Sahib and his Sepoys. The officers were shot, and their wives, daughters, sisters and babes, 206 in number, were shut up in a large apartment which had been used by the ladies for a ballroom.

After eighteen days of captivity, the horrors of which will never be known, five men with sabres, in the twilight, were seen to enter the room and close the door. There were wild cries and shrieks and groans. Three times a hacked and a blunted sabre was passed out of a window in exchange for a sharper one. Finally the groans and moans gradually ceased and all was still. The next morning a mass of mutilated remains were thrown into an empty well.

The Evolution of an Empire

Two days later the avenger came in the person of General Havelock. The Sepoys were conquered and a policy of merciless retribution followed.

In that well at Cawnpore was forever buried sympathy for the mutinous Indian. When we recall that, we can even hear with calmness of Sepoys fired from the cannon's mouth. From that moment it was the cause of men in conflict with demons, civilization in deadly struggle with cruel, treacherous barbarism. We cannot advocate meeting atrocity with atrocity, nor can we forget that it was a Christian nation fighting with one debased and infidel. But terrible surgery is sometimes needed to extirpate disease.

Greed for territory, and wrong, and injustice may have mingled with the acquisition of an Indian Empire, but posterity will see only a majestic uplifting of almost a quarter of the human family from debased barbarism, to a Christian civilization; and all through the instrumentality of a little band of trading settlers from a small far- off island in the northwest of Europe.

CHAPTER XIV.

[Sidenote: Atlantic Cable, 1858.]

But there were other things besides famine and wars taking place in the Kingdom of the young Queen. A greater and a subtler force than steam had entered into the life of the people. A miracle had happened in 1858, when an electric wire threaded its way across the Atlantic, and two continents conversed as friends sitting hand in hand.

[Sidenote: Daguerre's Discovery, 1839.]

Another miracle had then just been achieved in the discovery of certain chemical conditions, by which scenes and objects would imprint themselves in minutest detail upon a prepared surface. A sort of magic seemed to have entered into life, quickening and intensifying all its processes. Enlarged knowledge opened up new theories of disease and created a new Art of healing. Surgery, with its unspeakable anguish, was rendered painless by anaesthetics. Mechanical invention was so stimulated that all the processes of labor were quickened and improved.

[Sidenote: First World's Fair, 1851.]

In 1851 the Prince Consort conceived the idea of a great Exposition, which should under one roof gather all the fruits of this marvellous advance, and Sydenham Palace, a gigantic structure of glass and iron, was erected.

In literature, Tennyson was preserving English valor in immortal verse. Thackeray and Dickens, in prose as immortal, were picturing the social lights and shadows of the Victorian Age.

[Sidenote: Death of Prince Albert, 1861.]

In 1861 a crushing blow fell upon the Queen in the death of the Prince Consort. America treasures kindly memory of Prince Albert, on account of his outspoken friendship in the hour of her need. During the war of the Rebellion, while the fate of our country seemed hanging in the balance, we had few friends in England, where people seemed to look with satisfaction upon our probable dismemberment.

We are not likely to forget the three shining exceptions: —Prince Albert—John Bright—and John Stuart Mill.

[Sidenote: Suez Canal.]

It was while that astute diplomatist, Disraeli (Lord Beaconsfield) was Prime Minister, that French money, skill and labor opened up the waterway between the Mediterranean and the Red Sea. It would never do to have France command such a strategic point on the way to the East. England was alert. She lost not a moment. The impecunious Khedive was offered by telegraph $20,000,000 for his interest in the Suez Canal, nearly one-half of the whole capital stock. The offer was accepted with no less alacrity than it was made. So with the Arabian Port of Aden, which she already possessed, and with a strong enough financial grasp upon impoverished Egypt to secure the right of way, should she need it, England had made the Canal which France dug, practically her own.

[Sidenote: Victoria Crowned Empress of India, 1876]

Lord Beaconsfield had crowned his dramatic and picturesque Ministerial career by placing a new diadem on the head of the widowed Queen, who was now Empress of India. His successor, William Ewart Gladstone, the great leader of the Liberal party, was content with a less showy field. He had in 1869 relieved Ireland from the unjust burden of supporting a Church the tenets of which she considered blasphemous; and one which her own, the Roman Catholic, had for three centuries been trying to overthrow. We cannot wonder that the memory of a tyranny so odious is not easily effaced; nor that there is less gratitude for its removal, than bitterness that it should so long have been.

[Sidenote: Disestablishment of Irish Branch of Church of England, 1869.]

The disestablishment of the English Church in Ireland was one of the most righteous acts of this reign. Whether the great English Statesman will be equally successful in securing Home Rule for that unhappy land, upon which he has staked the final effort of his life, remains to be seen.

The Evolution of an Empire

The Irish question is such a tangled web of wrong and injustice complicated by folly and outrage, that the wisest and best-intentioned statesmanship is baffled. Whether the conditions would be improved by giving them their own Parliament, can only be determined by experiment; and that experiment England is not yet willing to try.

History affords few spectacles of its kind more impressive than Mr. Gladstone at 86, with the ardor and energy of youth, battling for a measure he believes so vitally necessary to the Nation. It is a pity that for Americans his greatness is tarnished and belief in the infallibility of his judgment shaken, by the memory that he upheld the attack upon our National life in 1860; and that he, seemingly without regret, prophesied our downfall.

The work of Parliamentary reform commenced in 1832 has moved steadily on through this reign. By successive acts the franchise has extended farther and farther, until a final limit is almost reached; and side by side with this has been a corresponding increase in educational facilities, "because, " as a Peer cynically remarked, "we must educate our Masters! "

So many reforms have been accomplished during this reign, the time seems not far distant when there will be little more for Liberals to urge, or for Conservatives and the House of Lords to obstruct. Monarchy is absolutely shorn of its dangers. The House of Commons, which is the actual ruling power of the Kingdom, is only the expression of the popular will.

We are accustomed to regard American freedom as the one supreme type. But it is not. The popular will in England reaches the springs of Government more freely, more swiftly, and more imperiously, than it does in Republican America. It comes as a stern mandate, which must be obeyed on the instant. The Queen of England has less power than the President of the United States. He can form a definite policy, select his own Ministry to carry it out, and to some extent have his own way for four years, whether the people like it or not. The Queen cannot do this for a day. Her Ministry cannot stand an hour, with a policy disapproved by the Commons. Not since Anne has a sovereign refused signature to an Act of Parliament. The Georges, and William IV., continued to exercise the power of dismissing Ministers at their pleasure. But since Victoria, an unwritten law

The Evolution of an Empire

forbids it, and with this vanishes the last *remnant of a personal Government*. The end long sought is attained.

The history of no other people affords such an illustration of a steadily progressive national development from seed to blossom, compelled by one persistent force. Freedom in England has not been wrought by cataclysm as in France, but has unfolded like a plant from a life within; impeded and arrested sometimes, but patiently biding its time, and then steadily and irresistibly pressing outward; one leaf after another freeing itself from the detaining force. Only a few more remain to be unclosed, and we shall behold the consummate flower of fourteen centuries; —centuries in which the most practical nation in the world has steadily pursued an *ideal*! The ideal of individual freedom subordinated only to the good of the whole.

The triumph of England has been the triumph not of genius, nor of intellect, but of *character*. It is those cross-threads of stubborn homely traits, the tenacity of purpose, the reluctance to change, the adherence to habit, usage and tradition, which have toughened the fabric almost to indestructibility. These traits are illustrated in the persistence of the hereditary principle in the royal line. We look in vain for another such instance. The blood of Cerdic, the first Saxon "Ealdorman" (495), flows in the veins of Victoria. She is 38th remove from Egbert, first Saxon King of consolidated England (802), 26th from William the Conqueror (1066), and 9th in descent from that picturesque and lovely criminal, Mary Stuart (1587). There have been wars, and foreign invasions, —a Danish and a Norman conquest, the overturning of dynasties, and Revolutions, and a "Protectorate, " and yet—there sits upon the throne to-day a Queen descended by unbroken line from Cerdic the Saxon!

Queen Victoria is undoubtedly indebted to the wise counsel and guidance of the Prince Consort in the early decades of her reign. Not one act of folly has marred its even current. She has held up to the nation a high ideal of wifehood, motherhood, and of domestic virtue. None of her predecessors have bound their people to them with ties so human, her griefs and experiences moving them as their own. We think of her more as an exalted type of Woman, than as Sovereign of the most marvellous Empire the World ever saw; —its area three times that of Europe, representing every zone, all products, and every race!

The Evolution of an Empire

How long England will be capable of sending out a vital current sufficient to nourish such distant extremities none can tell; or whether the far-off Colonies of Australia, Canada, and New Zealand will increase their independent life, until they become detached Sovereignties like the United States. If that day ever comes, like the Mother of a generation of grown children, with independent homes of their own, —England will sit with folded hands, her life-work done.

Let no American forget, that England before the Restoration is as much our England as theirs. That the memories of Crecy, of Blenheim, of Marston Moor and Naseby, are our great inheritance too. That Chaucer, Milton, Shakespeare, belong to the humblest American as much as to Victoria.

The branch has grown far from the parent tree since the 17th Century; and the England of Tennyson and Herbert Spencer is only a very distant cousin. She has not always treated us well, has not been chary of criticism, nor prodigal of praise, nor did she sympathize with us in the day of our peril and misfortune. But for all that— sharing the same great heritage of race and of literature, speaking in the same language the same thoughts and impulses, there must always exist between us a tie, such as can bind us to no other nation upon the earth.

Lightning Source UK Ltd.
Milton Keynes UK
UKHW011854100122
396910UK00002B/306